TACTICAL WISDOM

I0830663

FIELDCRAFT

TW-02

Tactical Wisdom

www.tactical-wisdom.com

COPYRIGHT © 2021 Joseph W Dolio

All Rights Reserved

ISBN-13: 9798527464382

Cover Art: Andrew Dolio

FIELDCRAFT

TACTICAL WISDOM SERIES

TW-02

JOE DOLIO

Preface

Neither I nor my brothers, nor my men, nor the guards with me
Took off our clothes; each had his weapon,
Even when he went for water.

Nehemiah 4:23

As we consider what a Without Rule of Law situation will look like, we need to understand that Nehemiah's advice from a few thousand years ago is still pretty solid. In the quote above, he's saying that he and his men were always ready for hostile contact, even when sleeping or getting water. That's solid advice.

It's easy to decide to buy some extra food, a couple gallons of water, and a whole bunch of expensive, ultra-cool-guy tacti-cool gear, and consider ourselves prepared. What you need more than that gear, though, is SKILLS. You can't carry all that stuff anyway. You can't lose skills and they never run out of batteries.

This book will bring you a set of skills that will be needed. Those skills are the ability to move and live in a hostile environment, using movement and security skills to stay safe in a WROL situation.

What will a WROL world look like?

First, we need to understand that there will not be police or fire/rescue personnel just awaiting your call. Many think that this is an outrageous claim to make, but is it?

We are already seeing that due to protests and rioting, law enforcement and fire services are stopped for most of the city in some areas, like Portland, Seattle, or Minneapolis. When things fall apart, these services, particularly law enforcement, will pull back and secure government facilities or "critical infrastructure" like hospitals.

In early 2021, we saw rioting in Brooklyn Center, Minnesota. There was widespread looting and crime. The police response was to drive around with their sirens on, in hopes of scaring off looters. That's the entirety of their response. What do you think the response would be if the looting was nationwide?

Many think that's a far-fetched idea. We actually had it in the first few weeks after the George Floyd incident. It's not at all unrealistic.

I frequently point out the examples of the Ukraine and Georgia. Those are directly relevant. Both faced a WROL situation and most of those areas are still that way today.

In Georgia, despite the large-scale fighting being over within 10 days, vast parts of the nation are still occupied by either Russian troops or ethnic Russian militias today. What do you imagine life is like for an ethnic Georgian, being hunted and harassed by militias and foreign troops daily for years?   That's where fieldcraft comes in.

The Ukrainian revolution was over in 72 hours, and all fighting was contained in the Capitol region. People in the rest of the country went about their daily lives with no real worry, because it was just "those kids protesting again". Right up until they woke up one morning with a new government ran by extremists.

Militias sprang up immediately to fight the new government and amid that chaos, the Russians invaded. Now, there are at least 4 different major armed parties fighting over the eastern half of the country, and dozens of armed criminal groups taking advantage of the chaos. People are daily out searching for food & water, while dodging patrols & checkpoints from every side.

Having the skills to move safely, live in the field securely, and provide for your own protection are vital in these areas. That's where fieldcraft comes in.

Here, we face the potential for a "Balkanization", or a breakup of the United States into various regions along racial, ethnic, and socio-economic lines. We face daily the threat of a breakdown of law and order.

This book is meant to assist in learning basic fieldcraft skills to enable prepared people to move and live in a hostile environment in the most secure way possible.

Veterans will recognize a lot of basic techniques they learned in training, but there are additional things in here from other places as well. This book is not just a re-hash of "Combat Skills of the Soldier" or "Warrior Skills", although those topics are covered. We will cover a lot of techniques taught by Western militaries, some by private military contractors, and some that are just general woodcraft skills.

The book is designed to provide a basic to intermediate level of fieldcraft knowledge to both the untrained and the veteran, and it will serve as a great training resource for your preparedness group. It's also a great refresher for anyone else.

It's worth noting that difference between a high-speed special operations soldier and a basic infantryman is mastery of the basics. It's the exact same with martial arts. The more you work on the most basic of skills, the better you become overall. A Marine Scout-Sniper doesn't learn "secret" fieldcraft skills, he becomes an expert at a very select few of the most basic, by repetition.

Get out and practice the skills in this manual, both individually and as a team.

Table of Contents

Tactical Wisdom

Fieldcraft

Chapter 1

Fieldcraft & WROL

Go out into the hill country & bring back branches
From olive & wild olive trees, and from
Myrtles, palms, & shade trees to make temporary shelters.

Nehemiah 8:15

Fieldcraft is defined as the techniques involved in living, traveling, and observing, from a tactical standpoint, in the field.

As I read a lot of preparedness and survival books along my own journey, I noticed that there were not many books that discussed these skills. This is probably because most people who first wrote about preparedness assumed that their readers were all former military or just somehow had that knowledge.

The problem is that even among trained personnel, terminology and techniques vary. No disrespect to my Air Force cousins, but the individual movement techniques taught by a force that operates in a rear area are not necessarily the same as those taught by forward-deployed forces.

We also see differences based on various nation's forces. For example, what we in the US military call a high crawl, our Canadian cousins call a "Leopard Crawl".

The solution then is to develop a single, unified set of terminology and techniques that your preparedness group can all agree on and all train together on. That's where this manual comes in.

From a training perspective, whenever groups get together to train, everyone wants to go directly to tactics, rather than individual movement. Tactical team movement is made up entirely of basic individual movements and fieldcraft, unified to arrive at a goal.

We see the same thing in Martial Arts training – everyone wants to learn some new, advanced form, or self-defense technique, yet once a month when we train with Grand Master Drouillard (the first American to receive a black belt in Tang Soo Do), he makes us spend the first few hours on the basic white and yellow belt techniques, because that's the foundation for everything else. You can't become an ultra-high-speed cool-guy in all your tacti-cool gear unless you have a solid foundation in fieldcraft.

Your hundreds of hours of range time and tens of thousands of rounds fired at targets are absolutely worthless if you get shot by a bad guy from 450 meters away, because you had no fieldcraft skills.

Another important note is that if your team comes from a varied background, and you don't standardize these techniques, there is a risk of endangering your own people. If you assume that someone knows the proper way to negotiate a fence, they can put your team at risk by climbing over it upright, rather than sliding under it, or cutting the bottom strand. The same goes for observation skills.

Spend some time training on these basic skills. Further volumes, like Scouting & Patrolling, will expand on these basic concepts.

But why will I need fieldcraft if I intend to bug in? Because, as we discussed in the Base Line Training Manual, you may be forced to leave your main location. You will also, at some point, need to venture out to find food or water. More importantly, you will need to get out and observe what is going on around you. The best way to stay safe is to learn what is happening around you. You can avoid a lot of danger by maintaining an awareness of your local security situation.

Remember what we are discussing here: a WITHOUT RULE OF LAW situation. That means that you won't be able to call the police and have them arrive in 5-10 minutes, if a threatening group arrives. Your best defense may be to grab your Patrol/EDC bag & your Belt Kit and go hide in a wooded area for a few days, to return later, when it is safe. Alternatively, you could at least get out of the house and set up a position to watch what happens and defend from an unexpected spot, rather than being trapped inside.

Under these circumstances, it won't be enough to just want to be left alone. The fight will most likely come to you, and fieldcraft will give you the skills to either successfully avoid the fight or to prevail.

Consider it as the "militant farmer" concept. American pioneers were ready to fight off raids by criminals, Native American war parties, or even a pack of wolves. Having a basic set of movement, observation, and security skills will enable you to do that.

In their training manual on Fieldcraft, the Canadian Forces define it like this:

"Fieldcraft is made up of the individual skills and techniques used by soldiers in the field, which include movement, use of ground and camouflage in conditions of reduced visibility. These skills and techniques enable soldiers to maintain their own security while gaining advantage over the enemy."

-Fieldcraft, Canadian National Defense

Fieldcraft is distinguished from bushcraft, which are general outdoors and primitive living skills. The two complement each other and neither is a substitute for the other.

In a WROL situation, fieldcraft will be needed for even the most basic of tasks. If you venture out for water or to gather food, if you haven't paid attention to fieldcraft, you may end up gathering things for someone else who may take them from you.

I know what you're thinking: "But society will never degrade so far that I have to worry about armed violence everywhere I go". Read stories about the aftermath of Hurricane Katrina, or the Balkan War. Before the Balkan War, Yugoslavia was a modern nation. Now, it remains a dangerous and mostly lawless place, with ethnic violence common.

Consider what keeps most people from stealing in current society. We like to think that it's our great morality, but it's truly a lack of need, coupled with the risk of police intervention. If you remove the risk of police intervention, and increase the need drastically, society crumbles, and fast.

People who haven't eaten in two weeks will do things they would never otherwise consider. Even more so when their children haven't eaten. Then, when you factor in simmering ethnic and political differences, and the mental breakdowns caused by a lack of electricity (millennials will not fare well post-electricity), you begin to understand the urgency and need for common fieldcraft skills.

None of us, in the current situation, consider having an observation post watching the street approaching our house, but it will be critical post-WROL. You wouldn't dream of running a patrol through the wooded area and along the stream near your house now, because the risk is reduced, but in a WROL situation, that patrol will be vital a couple of times a week.

You wouldn't dream of sending a team 5 miles down the road to spend a 24-hour period watching the freeway approaching your area. Post WROL, you had better, because that's where your early warning of issues will come from. Refugees and bad actors will flow along the roads, so maintaining some type of overwatch is necessary.

Fieldcraft is also distinguished from Battle Drills, which are preset responses to a situation, like "React to a Near Ambush". It's far better to have avoided being ambushed at all by properly using fieldcraft and remaining undetected or detecting the ambush before they see you.

While we may not be trying to repel a Chinese invasion or resisting a tyrannical government, these skills would go a long way if we had to do either of those things. That's all we'll say on that topic (Wink/Nod).

I have a few reminders from the Base Line Training Manual before we move on.

- Just because we are in a WROL situation, it does NOT mean we abandon our own morality.

- Having said that, the Bible says, "You shall not MURDER", not "You shall not KILL". Self-defense isn't murder. Moses even killed in the defense of a third party before the Exodus & God still used Moses.

- PAPER is an overlooked preparedness supply. I have cases of Rite in The Rain paper for post WROL use. You will want to document your observations that you make using your fieldcraft.

- You should document the circumstances of any violent encounters that you have in case order is restored and the authorities decide to ask you what happened to the local chapter of the "Leroy Jenkins" gang, last seen attacking your house.

- Our ultimate goal is SURVIVAL, not combat.

Most of the skills that we discuss in this volume are physical. After learning them, get out and train on them, a lot. Physical skills require thousands of repetitions to become instinctive. Many of the ideas may also seem counter-intuitive, but they are drawn from hundreds of years of Western military experiences and have stood the test of time.

After you've learned a movement technique without gear, train wearing your belt kit, which you should always be wearing post WROL. Then, train the technique while wearing your patrol/EDC bag. The mechanics are different in each, and most post-WROL movement will be done in both the belt kit and the patrol/EDC bag.

The cautions about security may seem obsessive, but security will need to be a way of life in a WROL environment. Our modern society has had us surrender all personal responsibility to others. We need to take that back for ourselves. We are responsible for our own safety & security.

Training Standard

- Commit as a group to standardize fieldcraft practices.

- Train on individual movement techniques in all three gear profiles (no gear, belt kit, and belt kit & patrol/EDC bag).

- Hold regular training sessions focused on just fieldcraft skills.

Tactical Wisdom

Fieldcraft

Chapter 2

Survival Mindset

Do not be overcome by evil,
But overcome evil with good.

Romans 12:21

The most important element in survival, whether in wilderness survival, or combat, is MINDSET. Your mindset and will to win can contribute more to survival than any other factor. You must maintain a proper mindset, no matter what happens.

You must make the decision and determination ahead of time that you will prevail and that you will survive. In a WROL situation, there are no timeouts or do-overs. There can be no "bad days" with a poor attitude. Survival is at stake.

The will to live needs to be the foundation for the rest of our preparedness or defensive training, whether it's for a WROL situation, or everyday self-defense in our current world.

<u>Awareness – A Review</u>

Central to our mindset for survival should be awareness. As we discussed in the Base Line Training Manual, awareness is the foundation for preparedness. We can't be ready for or deal with situations that we weren't aware of.

As we go about our daily lives, we need to carry ourselves in the awareness mode known as "Condition Yellow". This means relaxed but aware & prepared. It means maintaining good situational awareness.

This is a good time to review Cooper's Color Codes, designed by LtCol Jeff Cooper of the United States Marine Corps. It's worth reviewing because it's a core principle of a preparedness mindset.

Code	Meaning
White	Unprepared & unready to take action.
Yellow	Prepared, alert, & relaxed. Situationally aware.
Orange	Alert to probable danger. Ready to take action.
Red	Action Mode: Focused on threat response.
Black	Panic – unable to effectively respond due to panic.

Condition Yellow means knowing where people are, where threats may come from, and where the best way out is, everywhere you go. It's as simple as noting all exits from a building, including non-obvious ones.

Imagine that you are at a restaurant with your family, and a protest erupts, with rioters coming in and robbing & assaulting guests. An unaware person could be trapped inside, but if you've noted where the door to the kitchen is, you can lead your family out and to safety before the crowd is too close.

In a WROL example, if you were working at your bug out location, and heard vehicles approaching, you could grab your EDC/Patrol bag and slip into the woods before the vehicles arrived, so that you could observe them from a position of advantage, rather than standing in the open waiting for them to roll up on you, putting everything you have at risk.

A survival mindset is also why we don't store all our supplies in one location. If we maintain one large warehouse, and a large force rolls up, forcing us to leave, we now have absolutely nothing but what was in our EDC/Patrol Bag or Ruck when we had to flee.

Survival Mindset

The United States Armed Forces, during "Survival – Evasion – Resistance – Escape" or SERE training, uses an acronym to properly frame a survival mindset. As defined in Field Manual 3-05.70 "Survival", the acronym is:

S	Size Up the Situation
U	Use All Your Senses/Undue Haste Makes Waste
R	Remember Where You Are
V	Vanquish Fear & Panic
I	Improvise
V	Value Living
A	Act Like the Natives
L	Live by Your Wits/Learn Basic Skills

This is a great reminder of the mindset needed to survive in a WROL situation.

There will be danger, confusion, a lack of solid news, and fear. Without a proper mindset, it will be easy to just give up and die. Remember why you bought this book, why you got into preparedness, and why you want to survive.

Keep Your Head in the Game

Despite what all the cool movies depict, most of life in a WROL situation will be monotonous and boring. You won't be running from adventure to adventure, righting the wrongs of a world gone mad, even if you name does happen to be Eli or Max Rockatansky (Mad Max for you uncultured people who don't know).

Most of your time will be spent seeking food and water, tending to your food and water, pulling security, or moving on foot, either patrolling or changing locations.

It will be very easy to decide to skip setting up a watch schedule "just this one time" or to walk directly down a road, "because we need to make up time & it'll be easier". It's exactly those times of complacency that will harm you, and that's exactly when Murphy decides to rear his ugly head and spring a deadly surprise on you.

No matter how monotonous or tedious it becomes, you must keep your head in the game and get into the habit of using Fieldcraft, or it's urban intelligence-gathering cousin Tradecraft (but that's a topic for another manual), every single time, every single day.

Another piece of keeping our head in the game is remembering what our role is. As a preparedness group or family, our role is as a local security organization. That's important to remember, because it's easy to envision yourselves as light infantry, there to go out and make contact with hostile forces.

While that may occasionally be necessary to maintain your security, it's not your primary role. That's an important distinction, because you may be tempted to seek out bad actors before they are actually a threat to you. That's dangerous because you would draw attention to your group and its location.

Our main goal and primary focus is survival and avoiding detection.

Recap

Maintaining a proper mindset & will to live is a key to survival and will lead to you wanting to use proper Fieldcraft, even when cold, wet, tired, and hungry, and that's when you need it most.

Remaining in at least Condition Yellow is a preparedness technique that you can immediately apply to every area of your life.

Training Standard

- Decide that you will prevail in any encounter.

- Memorize Cooper's Color Codes.

- Commit to maintaining Condition Yellow & be able to define that condition.

- Memorize the acronym "SURVIVAL".

Tactical Wisdom

Fieldcraft

Chapter 3

Movement Techniques

Rescue those being led away to death;
hold back those staggering toward slaughter.

Proverbs 24:11

At the heart of Fieldcraft is individual movement. The most basic skills involved in Fieldcraft are individual movement techniques. All other skills evolve from that point. We cannot just move, "staggering toward slaughter", we must use good technique. Team movement is nothing more than applying individual movement techniques as a team.

In this manual, we will extensively cover individual movement techniques, drawing them from Western Military training, whether it be US, British, Canadian, or Australian. These will seem familiar to many, because there are only so many ways to move over ground, but the purpose of re-hashing even the most basic of movements is to get your entire team on the same page with a standardized set of techniques and terminology.

Veterans may notice slight variations from what they learned, because we are drawing from several different sources, and only retaining the best techniques. I know, as a Marine it's hard to believe, but the way you were trained may NOT have been the best method.

One of the training problems we see in the preparedness community is a reluctance to train in anything other than a standing position. This comes from the fact that everyone likes to train on a flat range, and there are rules there, prohibiting you from running or dropping into the prone or kneeling positions.

I guarantee you that if you have a preference for only standing, you won't last long. You aren't John Wick, and this isn't a movie.

There is also a tendency to not want to get dirty during training by spending hours crawling around on the ground. I have some bad news…in a WROL situation, you will spend hours laying in the dirt, with little chance of doing the laundry at the end of the day.

I also recall one day training with a team at a private military facility in Moyock, North Carolina. We were doing vehicle cross-deck drills, where we were simulating a vehicle down during an ambush. One of our team members, when told to jump over a seat back into the rear of the vehicle, said "I'm getting old, I don't want to do that". How long do you think he remained on the team? How long do you think he'll survive when his vehicle is hit in an ambush and he needs to perform the technique?

Train for realism, not for convenience. Besides, training is more fun when you get dirty.

Learn to Love the Prone

In a situation in which you are trying to avoid being seen or avoid being shot, the prone position in your friend. The prone position keeps you out of the line of sight and enables you to use micro-terrain, like small depressions, to hide. Using the prone position, you can look from under fences, bushes, and fallen trees, and remain low.

Human beings are fundamentally lazy, and we generally look for other humans at our eye level. Psychology also comes into play because we look for expected objects in expected places, like humans walking and cars on a road.

We'll discuss this more in our chapter on Observation but understand that being in the prone position is a must, in a hostile environment and when trying to avoid contact.

You should remember this fact when building your belt kit and any chest rig you might use. Many people stack so much on their chest rig or the center front of their belt, that they can't get completely into the prone position, use a small depression for cover, or conduct a low crawl without digging a trench with their gear. Resist the urge to stack gear on your chest rig or plate carrier.

The first few movement techniques will involve movement in the prone position, but first, let's talk about how to change the direction you are facing when prone.

Turning in Prone

When facing one direction and you want to turn your body to the right, first ease only your upper body as far to the right as comfortable, but very slowly. Next, move your left leg as far to the left as you can, but remember to lift it off the ground so that you don't make a shuffling noise. Finally, move your right leg in line with your body. Repeat until you are facing the way you need to be. Do the opposite to move left.

Roll

When prone on flat or descending ground, sometimes rolling is the best way to move. This is not an uncontrolled roll down a steep hill, but a slow and very controlled roll from one covered position to the next.

First, select your next position. Whenever you move, have a specific spot to end in mind. Unfocused movement is a bad thing. Once you have the position selected, pull your long gun (if you have one) tight to your side and just roll laterally to the next position in a controlled manner, ensuring that you end the motion on your stomach.

You can't do the "roll" while wearing a backpack, so keep that in mind.

High Crawl

A high crawl enables you to move close to the ground and behind low cover. It's good for periods of reduced visibility, like night or rain.

If armed with a rifle, you can either cradle it in your arms or continue to hold it in a proper firing grip with your firing hand and cradle it with your weak hand.

Select your route before moving. Lift your body off the ground and rest your weight on your elbows and knees, but keep your knees well behind the hips, to keep your body from rising too high.

Move by moving alternate elbows and knees, remembering always to keep the knees well behind the hips.

While this seems simple, it takes a LOT of practice and fitness to be able to do it at will. You will need training to develop the specific muscles this technique uses.

Low Crawl

The low crawl is good for when the cover is very low, or when there is good chance of being observed if you were any higher. The low crawl is very tiring and makes noise as you slide along the ground, so it's not ideal for long movements or when very close to people you don't want to know you're there. It's also hard to maintain observation while low crawling, so stop to raise your head often.

If carrying a long gun, grab the forward sling swivel with one hand, and let the gun lay along your forearm while moving. Take care to ensure that your muzzle does not drag in the dirt.

Stay prone and reach as far forward as you can with both arms and draw your right leg up as far as you can. Pull with your arms and push with your leg, then repeat. Change legs often to avoid fatigue.

As you can see, if you have too much gear on your chest rig/plate carrier, you're going to end up digging a trench, so keep that in mind as you build your kit.

Creep/Kitten Walk

The US Marine Corps calls this Creep, and the Canadians call it the Kitten Walk. The US Army doesn't teach it, so draw your own conclusions (Sorry, Army vets, I couldn't resist).

This is nothing more than crawling, but with tactics and silence in mind. It's best used at night but can be used in moderate cover during daylight.

Crawl on your hands and knees but use your hands to clear spaces before moving your knees up to where you just cleared with your hands. Make sure your knee goes exactly where your hand has just cleared.

Clear alternating sides as you move.

While moving, think of how a cat moves, very slowly and very quietly. That's the goal with the Creep.

Back Crawl

The back crawl, as the name implies, is laying on your back to crawl under an obstacle, such as a barbed wire fence, or a downed tree.

Again, you'd have to remove your backpack to this, but you could pull it along with a cord if you needed to.

Lay on your back, with your head in the direction you want to move. If armed with a long gun, hold it lengthwise down the center of your body. That way, if you are crossing under barbed wire, the obstacle slides along the gun, not your body.

Move by alternating your shoulders and pushing with your heels. Resist the temptation to raise your knees to push more or move faster, they may hit whatever you are crossing under, and either get entangled or make noise.

<u>**Upright Movement**</u>

It may seem silly to discuss how to use upright movement, because we've all been walking since we were very small. We're going to discuss some techniques to help you move quietly or move safely when under incoming fire or potential observation.

There are a few basic caveats to foot movement:

1. Step OVER logs, never step ON them. You don't know what condition it's in and a breaking log is loud, and you'll end up on the ground, also loudly.

2. Never, under any circumstances, walk backwards. You can't see, you are unstable, and you will eventually fall or run into something. You also can't see the rest of your team.

3. If you need to observe behind you, walk in a sideways shuffle, without crossing your feet. Better yet, stop and watch backwards, then turn and move forwards, stopping again to look back.

4. If it can be avoided, never cross your feet. It's a sure way to fall, and Murphy or Karma will surely visit while your legs are crossed during movement, landing you on your face.

5. Pick up your feet. In modern society, people tend to shuffle along, looking down at their phones. Watch where you are walking and pick your feet up to avoid making noise or tripping.

Remember, in a WROL situation, the best tactic is it to not be detected at all by people we don't know. Going unseen and unheard is far more preferable than having to win an armed confrontation with whoever may be opposing us.

Patrol Walking/Night Walking

When walking while in a potentially hostile environment (and in a WROL situation, anywhere outside your own perimeter is potentially hostile), we want to move slowly and quietly.

When we discussed rucking in the Base Line Training Manual, we discussed not being so focused on speed. When people engage in "rucking" they're always pushing for speed, trying to do at least 4 miles per hour.

The US Marine Corps, who walk everywhere they go, when conducting a road march in full gear only expects Marines to travel on the road at 4 kilometers per hour, which is only 2.4 miles. When moving cross country, the number drops to 2.4 kilometers per hour, or about one and a half miles an hour.

So, our first lesson is to SLOW DOWN. We are going for stealth, and our ability to cover a long distance. Moving too fast tires us too quickly and is too noisy for our purposes.

There is a technique to stealthy movement, and it's taught slightly differently between US forces and Commonwealth forces (UK/Canada/ANZAC), but the basic principle is the same.

Walk in a slight crouch, keeping your knees always bent. This seems odd, because when we walk normally, our knees lock briefly on each step. We keep our knees bent to act as a shock absorber, to keep our upper body from bouncing, and to maintain balance if we must stop quickly.

Ever had to stop quickly when walking normally? You almost fall over because your base leg, the one holding your weight, has the knee locked, making you unstable. If you had kept your muscles engaged by not locking the knee, you could stop mid-step and still be balanced.

As you walk, keep your weight on the back leg. Use either the side of your foot (Commonwealth) or your toes (US) to check the ground in front of you, setting it down lightly to feel for any sticks or other things that will make noise. Then roll the rest of your foot down, putting the weight on the front leg and repeat.

If you feel something as you go to place the foot down, find another spot.

Remember to lift your foot high and take small steps when conducting this technique. It's very quiet in the woods.

It seems like a lot to remember and very confusing at first, but once you have the technique down, it becomes second nature, and you can move fairly quickly and remain quiet.

The Combat Glide

The Combat Glide is a USMC concept that isn't a walk, and it isn't a run. It's a rapid forward movement, that allows you to maintain a stable firing platform, should you need one.

It's the basic movement technique when you think contact is probable. It builds on the patrol walk.

Move forward like the Patrol Walk, but at a rapid pace without the foot checking the ground. In other words, move quickly in a crouch, keeping the knees bent. Be careful not to move too fast. When moving too fast, you will feel your upper body bounce, and that's what we want to avoid.

It can best be described as a fast patrol walk. Your upper body, by twisting at the waist, functions as a gun turret, allowing you to keep moving while engaging a target anywhere. The bent knees act as a shock absorber, giving you a stable platform.

The Rush

The rush is exactly what the name implies. It's a quick run, when under fire or observation, from one location to another. A rush should last only 3-5 seconds. The US Marines teach this by making you say out loud as you do the rush "I'm up, he sees me, I'm down." That memory aid keeps you from wanting to make your rushes too long.

First, select the location you want to end up in. We never make unfocused upright movement when under hostile observation or fire. Have a plan FIRST.

Next, put your support hand under your shoulder and bring your legs up, ready to leap up. Push off with the support hand (your weapon should be in your primary hand) and both legs as you begin your rush.

Stop either just to the left or right of your intended destination. This is important, don't drop directly into the next spot. Drop to the ground, catching yourself with your toes and your support hand, kicking your feet out behind you.

End the movement by executing a side roll into the position you want to end up in. The reason for this is that anyone intending to harm you will fire into the spot where you dropped to the ground. You roll so that you aren't still there when they fire.

Another reason for the roll is that if they decide to wait until you get up and move again, they'll be watching where you hit the deck, not where you ended up.

Another caveat to this is that if you fired from a position, you should roll away from it before popping up to begin your rush. That way, anyone aiming at your location waiting for you will be watching the wrong place when you pop up.

Monkey Walk

This is a technique for fast movement over ground behind low cover or concealment. It's a way to move fast but remain low. It's very tiring, so it can't be maintained for very long.

It's essentially a three-point bear walk, or crawling on your toes and support hand, keeping low. A traditional bear crawl is crawling on hands and toes, in the Monkey Walk, we keep the support hand on the ground and our primary hand on the weapon system to move quickly behind cover or concealment.

Conducting a Stalk

The Canadians, in their manual "Fieldcraft", define "stalking" as the application of fieldcraft to eliminate the enemy. We define it as the application of fieldcraft to get closer to our objective without being detected. That objective may be something we want to observe, game if we are hunting, or hypothetically an opposing party.

First, locate exactly where the target is. Next, identify the spot which you want to get to for your objective, as these two spots may not be the same place.

Select a route before moving by considering any obstacles, cover & concealment along the way, any dead ground that you can use, and any areas you want to avoid (other people/animals that may notice you). Locate "waypoints" that you can use to ensure that you are still navigating on track, like a large tree or rock.

As you begin to move, remain alert and remember that fast movement attracts the attention of both humans and animals. Move slowly. Plan each new position before leaving the last one. Don't disturb any other wildlife in the area, particularly birds, as their flight attracts attention. Avoid obvious cover.

Following these tips should allow you to creep fairly close to your objective.

Individual Techniques Recap

These basic techniques will increase your ability to remain undetected or protect you from hostile fire should things get bad.

There are a lot of techniques in here, and you or your group may be tempted to pick and choose, but they are all taught to various modern militaries for a reason. Learn them all, and train on them all.

It's very easy to say, today, "I doubt I'll ever use the Monkey Crawl", but then in a year and a half, when trying to scoot across a rooftop and avoid be seen by a Chinese patrol in the mall parking lot, you won't have time to learn it.

Individual Movement Training Ideas

Learning these techniques will be difficult, but you can make it fun. A lot of them use muscles that we don't use every day in our modern, sedentary lives, so you need to practice the movements and exercise those muscle groups.

In this section, we'll cover a couple of training ideas that we used in our annual Tactics Training Camp.

Infiltration Lanes

Set up a course where students must move along a course using the different movement techniques, like a high crawl, then a low crawl past a low point, a back crawl under a barbed wire obstacle, then a rush over an open area.

With a little thinking, you can devise fun and challenging courses to get everyone to enjoy learning and using the techniques.

You can then set up a night infiltration course, where they use the same techniques, but try to remain quiet and unseen. We livened this up by having a few paintball gun armed snipers watching the course and firing near people who they saw and actually hitting those who were using terrible techniques.

You can use fireworks or pyrotechnics to make the course fun and entertaining.

A caution though – don't make the course demeaning or ridiculously demanding. Yes, military forces do, but they are generally dealing with young people who need to be broken down a bit. If you make your preparedness group crawl through the mud or a creek every time you train, they will stop coming. Yes, these things exist in real life and should be trained for, but don't use it every single time.

Unobserved Movement Course

Give the students an area to traverse, advising them that they will be under hostile observation. Your observers should have paintball guns or airsoft guns, some way of letting a student know they've been seen and hit.

The student must move from point A to point B without being observed, using proper techniques. You could run this either as teams or individuals, or both.

Taking this a step further, we had them move through a night patrol movement course, with our own fully camouflaged "snatch team" in the area. If the snatch team noticed someone using bad movement or falling behind, they snatched that person, as quietly as possible. It's fun when a leader thinks their team made it through, then you ask them to account for their team and they come up one person short.

Realism in Training

These are some fun exercises that you can run, and it will lead to some giggles, some laughs, and more than a few bruises (including bruised egos), but it's important to explain real life consequences at the end. In real life, you wouldn't have a bright yellow paintball stain; you'd be dead. Your captured team member would be tortured, killed, or both.

Have fun but explain what it really means in the end.

<u>**Training Standard**</u>

- Be able to perform the following individual movement techniques:

    o   Turning in Prone

    o   Roll

    o   High Crawl

    o   Low Crawl

    o   Creep

    o   Back Crawl

    o   Patrol Walk

    o   Combat Glide

    o   Rush

    o   Monkey Walk

Tactical Wisdom

Fieldcraft

Chapter 4

Negotiating Obstacles

Day and night they prowl about on its walls.
Malice and abuse are within it.

Psalms 55:10

For sure, when we come across an obstacle that we need to cross, we should heed that warning from the Ultimate Tactical Handbook that malice and abuse are prowling just on the other side of the obstacle. Keeping that in mind will cause us to be careful, which will keep us alive.

Obstacles are challenges to our secure and stealthy movement that require special techniques to cross in order to keep ourselves safe and hopefully unobserved. Things like wide-open areas, fences, walls, roads, and the like should all be viewed as obstacles.

We should always assume that obstacles are under observation. From a military defense standpoint, an obstacle only counts as an obstacle if someone is observing it. We don't know if the people doing the observation are friendly or hostile, and in a WROL world, that's a danger we need to mitigate. The best solution is the one I keep recommending, don't be seen.

In a WROL situation, we should be the ones determining who we make contact with, rather than blundering into other groups by chance. While you may bump into friendly groups, you'll eventually bump into a bad group. The best solution is to avoid everyone. Even friendly groups could become unfriendly when they realize that your supply situation is better than theirs.

Roads & Trails

Roads and trails mean people. People mean danger. In a WROL situation, roads will have patrols, both from whoever controls the territory (if anyone) and patrols of bad folks, looking for victims.

When approaching a road or large trail, find a covered and concealed place to observe it first. Watch for at least 5-10 minutes. Any shorter and you risk being caught in the middle of the road.

If there is regular traffic, try to find a way to cross under or over the road. Under, via a culvert or stream, is preferable, due to the risk of someone else using an overpass to watch the road. If crossing under by crawling through a culvert, be alert to the possibility of wildlife living in culvert, especially if you are in an area where there are alligators or crocodiles. Check thoroughly with a light first.

If there is no way to cross under or over the road, find a curve, rather than a straight segment of road to cross on. Have your team lay on the near side (where you are), with people covering both directions, and someone watching behind you.

Have a scout cross quickly and directly and immediately scout the far side for 50-100 meters in each direction. The scout then radios or signals the team and takes up a position covering the road.

You can now either cross as one large team, or as individuals, but cross quickly and directly. Once across, everyone takes up a position again and waits. Have people covering each direction on the road, one covering the way you came, and one covering the way you are headed. All-around security is vital.

As long as you aren't already evading someone following you, spend another 5-10 minutes observing where you just came from and watching the road. If you are being followed, the danger area you just crossed is a great place to spot whoever is following you.

You can also document whatever activity you see on the road to improve your overall situational awareness.

For small trails, find a curve or bend in the trail, and cross quickly as a team, after watching the trail for 5-10 minutes. Set up the same far side overwatch and watch for another 5-10 minutes before moving on. Your crossing may have alerted a group that decides to try and follow you, so watching is for your own security.

Walls

Walls are a danger area when we don't know what is on the other side. Walls are manmade, so there is a good chance that there are people nearby.

If you can, try to find a way around the wall, since going over the wall exposes you to being seen by your breaking the silhouette or skyline of the wall. If there is an opening in the wall, look through the opening for a bit first. If it can be avoided, never look over the top of a wall.

If you find an opening, observe through it for a few minutes, then send a scout through. As soon as you clear the opening, move either right or left of the opening and go prone to observe. If nothing is observed, signal the rest of the team. Each member should step through the opening and move either right or left (get clear of being silhouetted by the opening) and take a prone position covering their sector. Once the whole team is through, observe for a couple of minutes, then move out.

If you must go over the wall because there is no opening, one person goes over by rolling over the top as low as possible, rather than standing up on the wall and going over. After they roll over the top and lower themselves to the ground, they should take a prone position and observe. After determining that the area is clear, signal the rest of the team. Each person then rolls over the top and takes up a prone position covering a different sector. After observing for a few minutes, move out in the intended direction.

As you begin to move out, look for a covered and concealed position from which you can watch the wall you just crossed. Set up 360-degree security, and then watch the wall, to ensure that you aren't being followed.

Western military doctrine calls for blowing a hole in the wall if you don't find one, but we are not infantry, and we are trying to avoid contact and avoid noise.

Fence Lines

Fences are crossed differently depending on what they are made of.

Always approach a fence at an upright support. The support will give you something to observe around, hiding you from observation, and will give you the required support if you need to cut or go over the fence.

First, approach a fence at a support and observe the other side, while the rest of the team maintains security. Look for a place to cross under the fence without damaging it, if possible. That's the preferred method, as it leaves no sign of your passage. If you can cross under, each person low crawls under the fence, or back crawls if it's a wire fence, and then takes up a prone position on the far side of the fence observing their sector for 360-degree security. Don't forget to cover the way you came.

A note about wire fences: Check them visually for noise makers. Aluminum cans with pebbles in them make a very loud sound if there is any movement on the wire.

If the fence is chain link, barbed wire, or some other wire mesh type fence, and there is no way under, you may have to cut your way through. Be very careful here, because of noise.

We want to cut right next to a support beam, so that there is only an opening against the beam. The rest of the fence will remain tight with the method we intend to use. Hold the fence as you cut it to avoid the metal from springing away loudly and possibly injuring someone. Cut only enough for one person to pass through and never cut all the way to the top of the fence. Always leave at least the top strand intact, so that at a quick glance, it looks like the fence is still there.

After making the cut, wait and observe for a few minutes first. If you've tripped an alarm or set off a noisemaker on the far side that you couldn't hear, you don't want to be mid-crossing when a response team arrives.

After observing, have the team cross one at a time, and take up prone positions covering all sectors once on the far side.

Having a few zip ties in your pack can allow you to resecure the fence once you are through, to avoid the cut being detected.

A wooden fence should be crossed under it if possible. If you can't cross under it, treat it like a wall, and cross over it at a support beam, the same way you would a wall.

<u>Large Open Areas</u>

When moving through the countryside, large open areas can be very dangerous. You don't know who is watching them or who is on any of the sides. There are a few different ways to handle these, so we're going to handle each in turn.

Since we don't know who's watching, our first choice is to avoid crossing the open area.

The first method of avoidance is the contour method. Once you determine there is a danger area in front of you, your team can move just inside the wood line, skirting the open area by staying in the woods. You will follow the edge around the danger area until you get back to your original route. The problem with this method is that if anyone is observing the open area, they will also be just inside the wood line, and you will run into them if you aren't careful.

A way to avoid running into these groups is to use the offset method. Once you identify the open area, decide which side you'll go around. Take note of the bearing you are moving on (more on that in Land Navigation). Turn 90 degrees from the direction you are facing and move as team for a distance far enough to get around the widest part of the open area. Turn back to your original bearing and move far enough to cross the open area. Turn back 90 degrees toward your original route and move back exactly as far as you went on the first turn. Once you get there, finding the bearing of your original route and move out on that bearing.

Sometimes, the area is just too big to go around. Sometimes the only way is through.

You can send a scout or scout team across, just like we did with the road crossing, but when crossing a field of high grass or crops, avoid traveling in a straight line, as it's not natural. You perform this entire sequence exactly you did with the road crossing.

If it's a recently plowed field, you can low crawl through the furrows, in the lower part, and cross the furrows at the end of rows or at low points.

In North America and Europe, a lot of the larger open areas are farmland. They would take you too far out of the way to do either the contour or offset method, and the risk of the farms being occupied, as well as the size, precludes a direct crossing like a road.

In these areas, there are generally irrigation ditches, or drains with some vegetation in them between the fields. Your team can move along these, keeping yourselves below ground level and giving you a ready-made trench in case you make contact.

Before moving out on this type of route, observe and pre-plan your crossing. Expect it to take a long time and move slowly, always planning your next leg before moving out.

In a post-WROL world, it's important to note that farms will be considered a critical asset, and local groups may be staffing defensive positions and running patrols to protect their community food source. Expect to encounter armed overwatch from silos and the top levels of barns. As long as you keep moving, and don't approach the food storage areas, they should allow you to pass, but again, not being seen is the best route.

Crossing a Ditch/Trench

You may encounter a ditch that you just want to cross, rather than use for movement. Select a crossing point that has cover and concealment on both sides. If possible, cross at a turn in the ditch.

One person from your team should crawl to the edge and check the bottom of ditch and the far side for any obstructions. Cross the ditch quickly and quietly and then turn around and provide security for the rest of the team as they cross one at a time. As team members cross, they should take up positions covering 360 degrees. Once the whole team is across, move out.

Water Obstacles

If you come across a lake or a pond, you didn't do very well reading your map and planning your route to avoid it.

In all seriousness, bodies of water will attract humans, so caution is needed. When a lake or large pond is in your path, you will have no choice but to use either the contour or offset method described above under "Large Open Areas".

Small streams less than waist deep should be observed for evidence of human presence before attempting a crossing. Look for trails or footprints and watch & listen for people.

Find a shallow spot, preferably on a bend, and then cross just like a road or trail, as described above.

Crossing large rivers is a more advanced skill, that we will discuss in our Scouting & Patrolling volume. You should avoid them or cross them on a bridge or similar area.

Training Standard

- Be able to cross a road or trail.

- Be able to cross over or through a fence.

- Be able to cross a wall obstacle.

- Be able to conduct a contour movement around an obstacle.

- Be able to conduct the offset method around an obstacle.

- Understand how to cross a large open danger area.

- Know how to negotiate a ditch obstacle.

- Know how to cross a small stream.

Tactical Wisdom

Fieldcraft

Chapter 5

Observation

Be watchful, stand firm in the faith,
Be courageous, be strong.

1 Corinthians 16:13

For us to avoid being seen, we need to understand how human observation works. To "Be Watchful", as the Ultimate Tactical Handbook teaches us, we need to learn to observe what's happening in front of us.

First, we need an understanding of how things are seen. Learning this will help us be able to identify objects in front of us and help us to combat being seen ourselves.

- **Shape**: We see familiar shapes and associate them with our past experience. We all can spot a car, a train, or a person and we automatically associate the shape. You can do the same the same with shapes like rifles, backpacks, tents, and even a fighting position, if you have experience in viewing them. This is also the reason why we use camouflage to break up the outline of our gear, and our head & body.

- **Shadow**: We can identify objects by their shadows. Sometimes, an object or person may be concealed, but their shadow can be seen. Hiding in deep shadow is good, if you remain aware of where your shadow may be cast.

- **Contrast**: If an object contrasts with the things around it, it will stand out. This contrast can be color or texture. For this reason, camouflage or other clothing of an appropriate color should be worn. For example, I recommend wearing earth tones in a rural environment and gray or black in an urban environment.

- **Silhouette**: Silhouette is closely related to shape. Familiar silhouettes are associated with what we expect. Also, silhouette refers to silhouetting yourself against the skyline, open water, or a contrasting background.

- **Movement**: The human eye is attracted to movement naturally. When scanning, watch for movement. When moving, move slowly. The faster movement is, the easier it is to see.

- **Spacing**: In nature, you never find evenly spaced objects. Only man spaces things evenly. You can use this to identify man-made objects. It's also important to remember when moving or getting into positions, so that you don't present an evenly spaced appearance to observers.

- **Straight Lines**: Another thing that does not occur naturally are straight lines. Break up the appearance of any straight lines you may have (rifles, vehicles, tents). When scanning an area, look for straight lines where there should be none.

- **Position**: Human beings, based upon their experiences, associate certain things with the location where they are, even at great distances. For example, a box shape just off a road is house, a rectangle on a road is car. We look for familiar things where we normally see them. From a preparedness standpoint, that's why we avoid trails and roads.

- **Color**: Contrasting colors are another way in which we see things. Wearing bright colors in the woods stands out. Either wear camouflage or earth tones. This is also why I recommend finding a tent in an earth tone. Note: The color of blue jeans does not occur anywhere in nature.

- **Shine**: Metal objects and glass reflect light and cause shine that is visible for miles. Plan for this. You can cover optics with a shade or with netting. You can tie strips of burlap or cloth around firearms, as long as you don't interfere with their operation. Look for shine to identify other people who may be trying to spot you.

- **Noise**: Noise also draws the eye. When you hear a noise, you glance in the direction of it. Obviously man-made noises include conversations, radio static, metal on metal noises, etc. Strong noise discipline is vital. It's important to note that movement noises, unless very loud, are NATURAL. Animals move constantly. As long it's not obviously man-made like shuffling feet, or rhythmic like human footsteps, don't overly worry about a little movement noise. If you fall, don't shout, or call out. Lay still after a fall for a few minutes to listen. Vehicle sounds are inherently man-made.

- **Smell**: Another key piece of observation is smell. Man-made smells can be detected at great distances. Smells like cigarette smoke, smoke from a fire, cooking smells, or human body odors can be detected from farther than you think and only mean humans. Be aware of them and any smells you may give off. Always use fragrance free detergents, soaps, and deodorants.

These factors are the basic elements of observation. Paying attention to these as they relate to your own team will help you avoid detection. When you are observing an area or operating in general, these are the things to look for or pay attention to alert you to other humans.

Picking Spots to Observe From

While out moving, selecting the proper spot to observe from can prevent you from being seen while observing. Taking a few seconds to pick the proper spot can prevent a serious situation.

When observing from a hill, never look over the top. Remember silhouette from earlier. We call the very top the "topographical crest". Where you want to observe from is the "military crest", or the spot just below the crest where you can see the most, but you are not silhouetted against the crest.

When coming to an open area, remain inside the wooded area to view through vegetation. Learn to see "through" vegetation rather than moving vegetation to see. If you move it to see out, they can see in. Binoculars can be focused to see through vegetation.

If you are going to use some type of cover while viewing, like a rock, a log, or a fence/wall, view from around the end, rather than over the top. If you must observe over the top of a long wall, never break the straight line of the top. Look for a low point or damaged spot. Do the same with trees, looking around the base of the tree, as low as possible.

Whenever you pause movement in a wooded area to observe, which you should be doing frequently, understand that in the woods, stationary objects that are not trees are generally less than waist height. As a result, your observations should always be done while taking a knee, to appear low, like a bush. Humans also tend to look for humans at standing/eye level.

When observing from shadows, remember that shadows move with the sun. You may have been in the shadows an hour ago, but are you now?

When observing from within a building, remain well back from the window in the shadows. Remember that it is very hard to see into a darkened room from the outside of a building.

When observing around corners in an urban environment, lay down on the ground. Ease yourself slowly past the corner at ground level just far enough to see. We are using the tendency of humans to look for other humans at eye level. Slide back behind the corner when done.

Other observations from an urban environment should be done without exposing yourself over the roofline. We will discuss urban tactics later in the book.

Range Estimation

In a WROL situation, knowing how far away other people or vehicles are is essential, because you need to know how much time you have before they get to your position, or in a worst-case scenario, what range settings or holdover you need with your rifle. Having the ability to estimate range is a good thing.

The most basic method is the 100-meter (or yard) unit of measure. We can all envision a football field. That's 100 yards. When you add in the end zones, you're close to 100 meters (333 feet). Estimate the number of those units to the target.

Another method for longer distances is the "Halving" method. Locate a point halfway between you and the target, and then estimate the range to the halfway point. Then double that estimate to come up with the full range.

If you know the range to a particular object in view, like a house, or a road, you can estimate the target's distance from that object, and then add it to (or subtract it from) the known range.

Experience will also teach you the appearance of objects at various distances.

Training Exercises to Improve Observation

The best way to improve observation skills is to conduct training exercises with your team as the students. These exercises will help develop observation skills.

1. **Observation Stand**: This one comes to us from the British Royal Marines. Set several items out at various ranges in front of an observation stand, where students will stand to make their observations. The items should be things that will point out one of the observation points above like loose change or glass for shine, a backpack for shape, a person for familiar shapes, and a brightly colored item for contrast, etc. Allow students a short period of time to

observe the area and make a list and a sketch of the items.
As the students progress, you can increase the range.

2. **Kim's Game**: Place several items on a tray, and then
    cover them with a cloth. Remove the cloth and give the
    student a short period of time to observe, then cover it.
    The student then must describe whatever they can
    remember in as much detail as they can. As they improve,
    increase the number of objects. You could place a muted
    and dull object between bright objects, to reinforce the
    need to inspect in detail.

3. **Observation Lane**: Another Royal Marine exercise is the
    Observation Lane. Create a pathway about 100 meters
    long. Place objects or people conducting activities at
    various ranges on both sides of the lane. Include things
    that might rely on sound or smell, like a radio with traffic
    or a lit cigarette emitting smoke smell, along the path. At
    the end, the student prepares a detailed observation report
    of everything they saw, heard, or smelled along the lane.

4. **Daily Awareness Exercise**: Throughout your day, as you
    observe normal life, pause occasionally, and then write
    down everything you recall from the scene in front of you,
    including descriptions of people and vehicles, down to
    license plate numbers. This is how surveillance operatives
    are trained and can be a huge asset in developing general
    awareness.

5. **Detection Exercise**: Snipers all over the world use this
    exercise during training. Have the students attempt to get
    into a concealed position to observe where the instructor
    will stand. After they are all in place, the instructor stands
    and looks, trying to detect the students. If they are using

good positioning and concealment, they shouldn't be detected.

Understanding how observation works can help us keep from being seen and allow us to understand how to see others in a tactical environment. We should practice and develop our observation skills, while also training on how to remain undetected.

Spend some time training on these techniques and you'll find the skills improving, and they are fun exercises to conduct.

Training Standard

- Be able to list the factors of observation.

- Be able to select proper observation positions in particular environments (urban window, hilltop, wooded area, etc.).

- Estimate range within 25 meters/yards.

- Be able to traverse an observation lane without missing any objects/people.

Tactical Wisdom

Fieldcraft

Chapter 6

Analyzing Terrain & Routes

*He enabled him to travel over the high terrain of the land,
and he ate the produce of the fields.*

Deuteronomy 32:13a

When moving in a Without Rule of Law scenario, avoiding roads
and trails is a given, but there are other considerations as well. I've
mentioned several times that our role is not as infantry, trying to
gain contact with the enemy and maintain that contact. Our role is
survival & information gathering, so we want to avoid contact.

Knowing how to analyze the terrain from a tactical standpoint will
allow us to select the best route to avoid contact, and if contact is
made, allow us to maintain a position of advantage. Analyzing
terrain will enable us to select overnight camping sites that are well
concealed and that we can defend.

Don't worry, it's far less complicated than you might think.
Humans used to consider terrain this way instinctively. All we are
going to do is use an acronym to make it feel modern and super-
secret. It's not.

Frontiersmen, Native Americans/First Nations peoples, explorers, and soldiers throughout history have used this exact same process to pick out the best terrain to traverse to remain undetected or to set up positions and camps on. We're just going to give it a name and fancy acronym to feel more modern and educated about it.

KOCOA

I'm dating myself a bit, but when I attended Recruit Field Training Duty aboard Camp Pendleton, we used the acronym "KOCOA". Now, I see that the Army and Marine Corps, in true government fashion, took something easy to remember and decided to make it more difficult by changing it to "OCOKA", allegedly because some factors are more important than others. That's nonsense, they are all important.

We're going to use the easier to remember one, KOCOA, pronounced just like the wonderful winter treat, hot cocoa. First, I'll explain the acronym, then we'll drop down into a bit more detail on each point.

K	Key Terrain
O	Observation & Fields of Fire
C	Cover & Concealment
O	Obstacles
A	Avenues of Approach

KOCOA Terrain Analysis

1. **Key Terrain:** Key Terrain is any feature that gives one side an advantage if they control it. For example, if you want to know who is traveling along a road, a hill overlooking that road is key terrain. If you want to travel across a river valley, the high banks on each side are key

terrain. You must consider key terrain from both sides.
What may be key terrain to you, may not be to someone
seeking to ambush you. Essentially, it's any feature that
gives either side in a potential situation an advantage.

2. **Observation/Fields of Fire:** Observation is exactly what
    it sounds like, what can I see or what can be seen from a
    particular location. You must consider what can be seen
    from a particular location, and how that location might be
    seen from other areas. A hill might be great for
    observation along a creek, but if it can be seen from a
    higher hill, then it's not the best terrain feature.

    Observation is important because you want to be able to
    observe any Avenues of Approach to your position, and
    when you are selecting a movement route, you need to
    consider where you could be seen from.

    Observation is tied to fields of fire because you can only
    fire at things you can see.

3. **Cover & Concealment:** Concealment hides you from
    observation and cover protects you from fire. When
    selecting a position like an observation post or overnight
    site, you need to consider what cover and concealment is
    available. When selecting a movement route, concealment
    is the main concern, and you want to select a route that
    offers as much concealment/cover as possible. This
    usually means overland travel in thick vegetation; there are
    no easy ways.

    When selecting a location for a position or an overnight
    stop, consider what cover is available.

4. **Obstacles:** Obstacles are anything at all that stop, restrict, or slow down movement. When selecting a site, you want to look for obstacles that will impede people moving towards your position. When selecting a route, you want to find areas without obstacles in the direction you are moving. You also want to prevent entering any area with obstacles on both sides of your route; it's easier for you to be ambushed there and you won't be able to escape. Higher ground generally supports better observation.

5. **Avenues of Approach:** An avenue of approach is any area in which the above factors favor someone approaching your position or a place you want to go. For movement, you will find the best avenue of approach and use it. For defending your bug out location or any temporary site (like an overnight/over-day camp site), you want to post security watching the most likely avenue of approach.

There a few other terms related to terrain analysis that we need to define for later use. These are:

        A. **Topographic Crest:** The very top of a hill.

        B. **Military Crest:** The highest point of a hill that you can see down the whole hill. Because hills are almost never perfect domes, generally you can't see the whole slope from the very top.

        C. **Reverse Slope:** The back side of a hill. We are mentioning it here because you may choose to have your camp site on a reverse slope, with an observation post on the other side of the hill. This way, the observation post can alert the camp to anyone approaching and they can pack up to leave without being seen.

D. Dead Ground: Ground which you cannot see, but you can see all the ground around it. An example is a depression or a draw. If people enter the lower ground, you can't see them, but you can see all around them. The reverse slope of hills in front of you is also dead ground. In a WROL situation, dead ground is dangerous, and you should avoid using any site with dead ground around it. However, as long as you have a concealed way out, dead ground is a good place to use to hide or camp.

E. Natural Lines of Drift: This applies to areas in which humans will naturally move along. We are conditioned to follow roads and trails, but there are other natural areas that humans will instinctively follow for movement, and thus should be avoided. Rivers & streams are natural lines of drift. Millenia of humans needing water will have humans flocking along rivers. Another is a ridgeline. We've been conditioned throughout history that the high ground allows us to see better, so humans will walk along a ridge line (easier than climbing, too). Rail lines and along anywhere that the walking is easy are areas that you will encounter other people, and thus they should be avoided.

These are the most basic terms and concepts in analyzing terrain. You can use them for selecting a secure site, which we'll discuss in another chapter, or for selecting foot/vehicle movement routes.

Route Selection

Now that we have learned how to look at terrain from a tactical standpoint, let's apply that to selecting the best routes for movement. We'll begin with foot movement, as that's our main objective, but we will also touch briefly on selecting vehicle routes. A future volume of the Tactical Wisdom Series will cover vehicle operations in detail.

Route selection should really be done with a high-quality topographical map. Maps that show only roads don't show you hills, ridgelines, and terrain features. A "gazetteer" or "outdoor state atlas" type map is generally a hybrid road/topographical map, but they aren't exactly portable unless you tear pages out.

State Atlas Map Page

You can order topographical maps of anywhere in the world and order them printed on rain resistant paper. You can also download them from the National Geospatial Program on the internet (see Resources Section) and then have them printed at an office store on a large format printer. You can print them on your home printer, but they won't be very usable, as they will be very small.

Using a topographical map will enable you to apply the KOCOA analysis to the route. When moving, you want to avoid key terrain, avoid areas that give others good observation of your movement, use areas that give concealment, don't have obstacles, and use good avenues of approach.

You will want to note key terrain along the route because those will be danger areas. You may also want to identify key terrain with good observation for you to take a look at your surroundings to see what's happening from time to time.

While the planning the route, another good idea is to look for areas that you will pass that do have good observation of your route that you can't avoid. Those may be areas for your team to stop for a rest, form a concealed line, and watch to see if anyone is following along your route, while taking the rest or food break. Veterans will recognize this as setting a hasty ambush to "clean your tail", but that's a topic for another volume of Tactical Wisdom.

Don't select the easiest, most obvious route, like roads and trails, because those intent on harming others will be along those routes looking for victims.

The best route will be free from obstacles, offer at least concealment (and preferably cover), and give you good observation while denying it to others trying to observe you. This may mean that your route is twice as long as the most direct route. Our goal is never speed; it is always to avoid contact.

In a WROL situation, the people we are trying to avoid, whether they are hungry refugees or looters, won't be considering these factors at all. You will have a distinct advantage if you do.

A caveat to that is that if you are, for example, resisting a tyrannical government (completely hypothetical) or a Chinese/Russian invasion, rest assured that they are using this model, and you'll need to consider it from their point of view even more, while avoiding obvious avenues of approach. They will have ambushes set along them. But again, that's a purely hypothetical topic for another purely hypothetical volume of Tactical Wisdom.

Plan to cross any roads or streams at a bend and look for a key terrain feature overlooking that area, so that you can use the techniques described earlier for crossing a road. Plan to completely avoid open areas if you can. If you can't, try to find dead ground, like the irrigation ditches discussed earlier, to cross these areas, or just plan your route to use either the contour or offset method to go around them.

If there are any residential or urban areas, like towns or cities, either avoid them entirely by going around, or cross them carefully under cover of darkness. We should be avoiding them entirely unless absolutely necessary and well planned.

Planning Vehicle Routes

In a WROL situation, vehicle movement is less than ideal, unless necessary to cross large distances. Vehicles should not be planned on, because in any WROL scenario, fuel shortages or unavailability are second or third order effects. We just can't plan to always have our vehicle. Also, if we do have a vehicle, gasoline will be a finite supply, and we can't waste it on unnecessary vehicle movement, like security patrolling. Vehicles are also louder than foot movement and must generally follow known routes.

If you have vehicle-related WROL plans, you need a siphon pump. Hand operated models are silent and available anywhere auto parts are sold today. On day 3 of a WROL situation is not the time to be looking for one, because the looters will already have them all. They cost less than $10. The only addition I made to the one I purchased was longer tubing, to drop down into underground storage tanks. Electrical versions are available, but they cost more and are quite loud.

When planning any vehicle movement, we apply the same terrain analysis model, but consider that what may not be an obstacle to foot movement, could certainly be an obstacle to vehicle movement. You need to know your vehicle's ground clearance, to know how tall of an obstacle, like a curb, you can drive over.

Vehicle routes should avoid highways. They are called limited access routes because they are intended for government use during an emergency. You may encounter roadblocks and checkpoints on them, or at entrances/exits. People will also flock to them – they will be filled with refugees on foot and bandits/looters setting ambushes to prey on people using them. I realize this is the complete worst-case scenario, but we always plan for the absolute worst case.

Select roads that avoid built up areas. If there is a town on the map, locate a route around it. I know that many have no choice but to begin their route in a built-up area but find smaller surface streets that lead out of the area. In a WROL situation, whether a natural disaster or man-made, main roads will be clogged with people getting out of the city. Small towns will have checkpoints.

Try to cross major arteries and highways where you can cross over or under them. However, before going over or under any bridge, it's a good idea for a team (could just be two people) to dismount and check out the area around the bridge on both sides, just like any other danger area. You don't want to be ambushed and trapped under or on top of a bridge. The scouts need to take radios, scout both the near & far side, and then hold far side security positions, until your vehicles come to them and pick them up.

While analyzing the route for vehicle movement, consider areas where you could stop overnight if needed. WROL vehicle movement, contrary to what happens in the Mad Max series, will be much slower than you think. You don't want to be driving too fast to come to a quick stop to avoid a roadblock or ambush. A trip that normally took you three and a half hours (my journey to my bug out location), may now take you two days.

Select a spot where you would be able to pull the vehicle down a side road, away from your route, and preferably completely off the road, where you could cover it with a camouflage tarp. This is important, because desperate people will do desperate things when they've been walking for days and suddenly find a fully stocked vehicle. Cover the reflective windows at a minimum.

Have enough tarps to cover your car from casual observation in your car kit. You need to move at least 50 yards away from the car before setting up a camp site. This will give you the ability to defend the car from a better position, or if a larger group finds the vehicle, allow you to remain hidden.

Remove only the essentials from the vehicle when staying overnight. Just your patrol/EDC bag, belt kit, defensive tools like firearms, and your sleeping system. You want to able to run back to the vehicle and get away with minimum packing if necessary.

For planning vehicle routes, an outdoor state atlas type map is best, because it shows both roads and terrain, allowing you to select the best route.

Michigan Atlas

We will discuss full Post-WROL vehicle operations in a later volume of the Tactical Wisdom Series.

Training Standard

- Be able to recite the letters of KOCOA acronym.

- Be able to define what each letter means.

- Given terrain or a map, demonstrate how to select a proper tactical foot movement route.

- Given a map, demonstrate how to select a proper vehicle route.

<u>**Resources**</u>

1. Topographical Map Downloads
   a. apps.nationalmap.gov/downloader/#/
   b. https://www.natgeomaps.com/trail-maps/pdf-quads

2. State "Atlas/Gazetteer" Maps
   a. https://scmaps.com/
   b. https://buy.garmin.com/en-US/US/p/575993

Tactical Wisdom

Fieldcraft

Chapter 7

Establishing a Secure Site

*...To search out places for you to camp &
To show you the way you should go.*

Deuteronomy 1:33b

Since we won't have an Angel of God to go ahead of us and point out the best site for us like Israel had in the Ultimate Tactical Handbook verse above, we had better learn how to do this for ourselves. That's what we will do in this chapter.

We must remember the situation we are in. There is no Rule of Law, no help to come if people intent on bad things arrive in the night. That piece of awareness must be at the forefront when we are selecting a site to stay overnight or over-day if you are traveling by night.

In order to avoid falling into the familiar habits for picking out a campsite, we're going to stop calling it that. In the US forces, it's called a "Remain Overnight" or "RON" sight. The Commonwealth forces call it a "Lay Up Point" or "LUP". Whichever your group decides to use doesn't matter, just stop calling it "camping".

The reason is that we've been conditioned all our lives that camping is a laid back, relaxed, and fun activity, where we get all our stuff out, make a large circle of tents, and have a giant, roaring fire, all while singing songs and not worrying about things. We need to bury that attitude. There will be no S'mores in The Collapse.

Once we've nipped that in that bud, let's give a couple of reminders from the Base Line Training Manual about our outdoor gear.

1. Shelters must be SMALL. We don't want a giant, 3 room, cabin tent. A small, 3 person backpacking tent person is low profile, easy to carry, and is just the right size for one person and their gear.

2. Shelters must be camouflage or in earth tones. For safety reasons, tent manufacturers tend to make tents in bright and loud colors. If you look around, you can find them in earth tones, which are easier to camouflage. You could also put a camouflage tarp over the tent.

3. We don't NEED a tent. Tarps work fine, especially camouflage ones. Learn to make a lean-to or A-Frame with a tarp. Military ponchos work just fine as well.

Along with those, we are going to add a bit more tactical over-night knowledge with a few additional gear tips.

1. Sleeping Bags: Don't get a four-season bag. Get a three-season bag, and if it's colder than the rating,

add a wool blanket, a poncho liner, or wear heavier clothing. It's not worth the added bulk and weight.

2. Again, manufacturers seem to prefer bright colors, so shop around for one in camouflage or earth tones. Alternatively, you can buy a camouflage or earth tone bag that fits over the sleeping bag.

3. Early Warning Devices: You can buy trip wire alarms that you can place along likely avenues of approach. There are models that fire a primer with a loud noise or a blank shotgun shell. While these will alert you to someone approaching, remember that it will sound like gunfire and might provoke an attack. You could also make your own using trip wires or fishing lines, with empty cans filled with small pebbles.

<u>Selecting a Site</u>

The first step in establishing our secure site is to pick a good spot. Fortunately, the US Military has an acronym to help us. Acronyms make us sound cool when we're talking to our friends, so let's learn a new one to help select a safe & secure overnight site.

B	Blends in.
L	Low silhouette.
I	Irregular shape.
S	Small.
S	Secluded.

1. **Blends In:** The site should, when occupied, look natural and like it's part of the background from a distance. This is where

not having bright colors or giant tents helps, along with camouflage tarps.

2. **Low Silhouette:** We want to stay below the horizon. If you are setting up in low brush, but your shelters rise above the concealment, you will be easy to spot. We also want to stay below the topographical crest (very top) of any high ground.

3. **Irregular Shape:** If you lay out your site in neat rows, or a circle, it is obvious what it is from either overhead (drones are cheap and everyone has one), or from a slightly higher elevation like a hill.

4. **Small:** We are looking only for a site that can hold our group. It doesn't have to be a giant site. We want as small a footprint as we can possibly have. The bigger the site, the more likely it is to attract attention.

5. **Secluded:** You want to be as far from others as you can be. This means finding a site away from all "natural lines of drift", like roads, trails, streams, or any area humans might traverse. Being secluded allows you to remain undetected, and to hear if others are approaching.

These factors, along with the KOCOA factors, should enable you to select the best overnight site relatively easily. It seems like a lot to remember at first, but it takes PRACTICE. Get out now and train on selecting sites and setting up sites. There is a skill to it.

Securing the Site

Once we have selected a site, we need to do a quick sweep of the site. This is to make sure we can indeed use it, that it's not already occupied, and to look for any signs of human activity on the site.

One or two members (preferably two) enter the site, while the rest of the team provides security. The point they enter is what we will consider the 6 o'clock position. Imagine a clock face on the ground. They will clear in a zig-zag pattern, first from 6 to 3, then 3 to 9, and finally 9 to 12, and then returning to 6. This is a quick, yet detailed search, to make sure that the site is unoccupied and hasn't been used by anyone else.

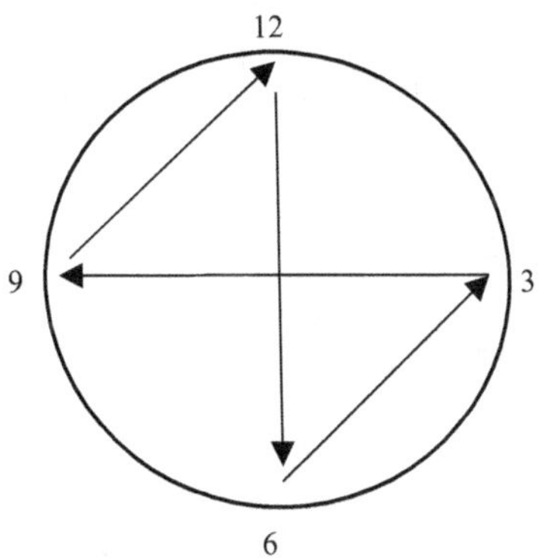

Securing the Site

This is a vital point. If the site has previously been used, the last group may return, or someone looking for them may come along. You also don't know how they handled field sanitation, and in a WROL situation, disease is a real concern.

Once you have checked the site, and decided it is good, bring the rest of the team in and place them all in their own areas, facing outboard. No one sets up shelters yet.

While the rest of the team is facing out in a security posture, with good cover and concealment, send one or two people to circle the site about 50-100 meters out. This is done to make sure that no one else is set up near your site.

Once your patrol returns, you can have half the team stay on security while the other prepares, eats, and then cleans up from their meal. Switch roles. Do the same thing with setting up shelters/sleeping systems. One half works, while the other half maintains security.

This is the pattern for all over-night site routines, half on security, half working.

Stand-To/Security Posture

Dusk is the most dangerous time. A light sky and darkened ground make it harder to see.

Establish a 100% security alert, or "Stand-To" from one half hour before sunset to one half hour after, and from one half hour before dawn to one half hour after. During this, everyone is facing outward, watching their sector with their personal defense weapon in the prone position behind good cover and concealment.

When you go to a Stand-To, whether the twilight ones or because of a potential threat, don't call it out loudly. Someone should walk around to wake those sleeping quietly.

Establish a clear watch schedule for the night. If your team is less than 8 people, than you can assign one person to security at a time, but they will have to be watching all directions, while focused on the main avenue of approach. With more than 8, you can assign people to 2-person shifts. Each shift should last no longer than one hour.

I know some veterans will say this is too little for security, but we are talking about a team avoiding contact, not a combat patrol. We will address combat patrolling in another volume. Here, we are focusing on elementary fieldcraft for a preparedness group, not a full-on recon patrol or combat patrol.

Having said that, remember that security must be your number one focus in a WROL situation. Err on the side of too much security, rather than letting it slide "just this one time" …. there may not be a next time if you do.

Site Routines

When we are in an overnight or over-day site, remember we aren't camping. Everyone must be accounted for at all times and there are no solo "wandering" expeditions. The best way to avoid this is to keep moving until about an hour before dark and leave the site less than an hour after sun-up.

No one can go anywhere alone. When sending out a water party to fill canteens (we'll discuss purification in the Field Sanitation chapter), or to use the latrine (Field Sanitation chapter), at least two people go together. One for the task, and one for security. Both should be armed. They should also continue to use fieldcraft and both should have a radio.

Establish just a few paths around the site, called "rat-lines", to avoid leaving signs and clearing brush all over the site. Using only a few paths prevents anyone who inspects the site from determining exactly how many people used the site.

Before leaving, check for obvious signs that the site was used and try to camouflage them with leaves or other forest debris, but don't cut new branches. Also, ensure that your latrine area is filled in and camouflaged, as well as any other holes dug.

Any cooking fires should be out before dark. Many sources say only have a cold camp, and I would agree for a full-on combat patrol, but if it's just a group moving, cooking fires would be OK before dark, just not large ones.

The reason is that in a WROL environment, the smell of woodfires for cooking would not be unusual and you usually can't locate a site by that smell alone. The bright fire after dark, however, would be a beacon that draws attention to your exact location.

Here are a few points on site routine paraphrased from the Australian SAS, in their rules titled "Lead Scouts and Jungle Soldiers":

1. Your rifle should never be more than an arm's length away from you, even when eating, sleeping, or sitting. It should never be out of your sight.

2. You should be wearing your Belt Kit at all times. When sleeping, it should be within arm's reach.

3. Put up your shelter just as it gets dark and be packed and ready to move at first light.

4. Check your site for any signs left before moving out.

5. Try to select a site when a surprise night attack would be impossible.

6. While in the site, any gear not in immediate use is kept secured in your pack/ruck.

Measures to Enhance Security

There are a few things you can do to enhance your overall security, if the risk level of facing advanced opposition, such as a hypothetical Chinese invasion, or hypothetically resisting a tyrannical government, is elevated.

Have all shelters/personnel under overheard cover, whether its trees or brush. This should prevent a drone from seeing your personnel or shelters.

The use of thermal tarps is a good idea. US issue casualty blankets are OD on one side and heat reflective on the other. You can also find "survival blankets" that are heat reflective on one side and camouflage on the other. Suspending this above a shelter or individual fighting/observation position would hide it from thermal detection methods.

Using night vision is good but understand that it works both ways if you use the IR illuminator to cast a beam. A better solution is to use night vision to detect others using night vision. Leave yours in the passive mode, with the IR beam off. By looking through the passive lens, you will be to see anyone else using active IR illumination. Anyone using night vision approaching your position is a BAD sign.

The security team or person should have passive night vision at all times.

Your team could set up an observation post with at least two people back where you left the trail to watch for anyone following. They could radio the site if they saw anyone.

The final additional layer is radio detection. You could have a radio always scanning the FRS/GMRS frequencies while you are in a static location. Those are the most common radios for civilian use in North America (you could scan PMR in Europe, or whatever your local "Free-Net" system is). Anyone using radios while moving at night should put your group into an alert status.

Training Standard

- Maintain proper field gear, including shelter and sleep system.

- Be able to recite & explain the BLISS acronym.

- Demonstrate the proper method to clear and secure an overnight site.

- Describe the Stand-To procedure.

- Be able to explain the overnight site routines.

Tactical Wisdom

Fieldcraft

Chapter 8

Field Sanitation

He will bring on you all the diseases of Egypt that you dreaded,
And they will cling to you.

Deuteronomy 28:60

In a WROL situation, there are no hospitals or urgent cares. If they
are still running, they will be filled with more risks than not going
would present. They will be filled with sick people and probably
overwhelmed, and the risk of infections and epidemics near
hospitals will be great.

For this reason, we need to take every possible step to ensure that
we are keeping ourselves safe from illness. Living in the field
raises the risk, but there are steps that we can take to limit that risk.
We call those measures "Field Sanitation".

Understand that a lack of field sanitation can cause serious illness
or death, and a very unpleasant death at that. We always prepare
for the worse case, which is no hospitals to treat the sick.
Carelessness in these areas is what causes illness. Keep that in
mind, as we discuss field sanitation procedures.

The first understanding your team needs is that sanitation & hygiene is everyone's responsibility. Each person should always maintain at least a 90-day supply of personal hygiene gear.

Personal Hygiene Gear List:

- Hand Sanitizer (Alcohol Based)

- Scent free deodorant

- Dental kit with toothbrush and either powder or paste. You can just use a brush with water.

- Powder (both foot and body, unscented)

- Comb/Hairbrush

- Lip balm

- Unscented Soap/Shampoo

- Sunscreen

- Insect repellent

- Small towel/washcloth

- Shaving Kit (razor at a minimum)

- Toilet tissue (flushable wipes are good and biodegradable)

You should store this entire kit in some type of bag, so that you can readily transfer it between any bag you are carrying (like from the Patrol/EDC Bag to the Full Ruck).

These things should be considered now, before a WROL event. For example, have you considered what you will shave with in a WROL situation? If you use either disposable razors or disposable blades, what is your resupply plan? Will you stock hundreds of blades or razors? For me, the solution is easy, go look at history. The old-school straight razor is no tech. You can use it for decades without replacing a blade if you take care of it. It also doubles as a weapon way better than a disposable razor does.

Personal Hygiene

Everyone should shower or bathe daily if possible, but at least once a week when in the field. Camp Showers are a great alternative in a WROL situation. They are sold at outdoor stores. It is essentially a black bag that holds water, that you can hang in a tree. The sun warms the water in the bag, and it has a hose and showerhead attached. In the field, you set up a field shower area, just ensure that it is away from sleeping areas and food preparation areas. Remember that two people must go anywhere together.

You can just clean with a wet washcloth or hygiene wipes if needed but pay special attention to folds and creases in the body when cleaning.

Use hand sanitizers or wipes before eating.

Undergarments should be moisture-wicking and changed daily, while outer clothing can be changed weekly. If you can't launder your clothes in the field, you can crumple them up, then shake them out, and hang them in the sun for a few hours to refreshen them.

Socks should be changed regularly, including as soon as possible if they get wet. You can hang wet socks from your pack to dry them and air them out while moving.

Oral hygiene is important as well. Teeth should be brushed twice a day. You can brush without toothpaste, but make sure you rinse the toothbrush after and store it in a ventilated container. Chewing gum is a good way to help maintain dental health as well. If you don't have a toothbrush available, you can wrap a small piece of cloth around your finger and use that to scrub your teeth.

Water Supply

Any water that is not from a known and trusted source should be treated as potentially dangerous. It should be treated before being used for drinking, cooking, brushing our teeth, or washing (pathogens can enter cuts or other places).

Bringing water to a rolling boil for at least one minute meets World Health Organization guidelines for water safety. Whenever we have the capability, we should use boiling, because it doesn't require the use of any limited supplies we might have.

Another good option is a water filter. There are many types and styles available, and each has its own strong points. Select one that works for you and learn to use it. Filters, however, frequently require a substantial time investment, so keep in mind that. It will require you to remain in a location for longer than you might want.

Some filters, like the Sawyer Mini I use, can be attached as an inline filter for use with your own hydration bladder, allowing you to quickly grab a full bladder of water and filter it as you drink. Remember that if you do this, you need to sterilize your bladder afterwards.

Purification tablets, which are available at outdoor stores or in the camping section of most superstores, are a good option for while on the move as well. For a standard 1-quart canteen, you can fill the canteen, drop in 2 tablets, and start moving. After 5 minutes, loosen the cap and shake the canteen up, and continue on your way. The water is drinkable after 30 minutes. Current versions also come with "neutralizing agent" tablets to reduce the chemical smell or taste. After the first 30 minutes, drop in the same number of tablets and wait at least 3 minutes.

You can use purification tablets with a hydration bladder as well, you just have to change the dosage.

Container Size	Number of Tablets
Canteen – 1 quart	2
Canteen – 2 quart	4
Bladder – 70 oz.	4
Bladder – 100 oz.	6

Every time you pass a water supply, you should completely restock any water used, unless you are under pressure and must keep moving.

Remember, though, security. Before filling up at any water location, watch first to ensure that no one else is getting water. Then, one member of the water party provides security overwatch while the others fill up containers.

If you are carrying canteens on your belt kit, and a water bladder in or on your pack, a good practice is to refill your canteens from the bladder and drink from your canteens. This way, it keeps the water in the smaller containers, and enables you to have a larger, faster filling container for resupply and chemical treatment.

<u>**Managing Waste**</u>

When in the field, human waste is big concern for illness prevention.

As soon as you decide on an overnight/over-day site, locate, and designate a latrine area at least 30 meters (66 feet) away from the main site. Again, no one goes there alone. This site should be down-grade from the site (downhill). The latrine area also needs be at least 30 meters (66 feet) from any water source and downstream from where you conduct water re-supply or washing.

For field use, you will dig a cat-hole latrine. This is simply a hole dug 6-8 inches deep and 4-6 inches across, for a single person. After use, fill the hole back in. If you are using biodegradable toilet paper or wipes, you can leave them in the hole when you cover it.

For use by the entire team, dig the hole deeper. After each use, each person puts some dirt back into the hole, to keep odors down and bugs away.

Before leaving any site, ensure that the latrine area has been refilled and camouflaged.

Do not allow team members to urinate inside the site. They must go to the latrine site. Allowing people to urinate all around a site will lead to illness.

<u>**Recap**</u>

Field sanitation is always important, but in a WROL situation, it's a matter of life & death. Make these practices a part of your training routine and insist on 100% compliance. An illness could spread through your entire team.

Training Standard

- Stock and maintain a personal hygiene kit.

- Demonstrate the ability to dig a cat hole.

- Describe at least two methods of water purification.

- Be able to explain how to properly site a latrine area in reference to sleeping areas and water sources.

Tactical Wisdom

Fieldcraft

Chapter 9

Camouflage

When the wicked rise, men hide themselves.

Proverbs 28:28a

When we say "camouflage", people immediately think of clothing or colors. Camouflage is actually an activity that clothing and colors either contribute to or hinder. In this chapter, we are going to discuss how to mesh the two together.

Whenever I start discussing camouflage and it's use for WROL, invariably some internet expert decides to inform me that "gray man" is far superior to camouflage. While we will indeed discuss Gray Man tactics in another chapter, I contend that Gray Man is for urban intelligence gathering, not survival. And, in a rural area, there is nothing more "gray man" than never being seen in the first place.

In a WROL situation, any person who sees you isn't going to care what you are wearing, they will know that other people mean food and supplies. A far superior plan to looking unremarkable, is to be completely undetected through the proper application of camouflage and fieldcraft.

A side benefit is that if people intent on bad things see a group of people moving carefully in full camouflage during a WROL situation, they will think "that's a military unit and I'm not messing with them". Take every advantage you can get.

Camouflage is the art of blending with your environment to look like something other than what you are. Blending in with the background, breaking up your outline, and moving carefully will help.

Clothing

If we're talking about blending in because we are accomplishing some task in a rural setting, like a local security patrol, hunting, or just moving to or from our bug out location, camouflage is king. We're going to discuss how to select the proper camouflage pattern for your area, but let's first address people who resist this idea.

You can wear earth tones, like khaki or green, and be "OK", but if you truly want to disappear and be safe, camouflage is the way to go. I recently discussed just wearing solid green with some people, but what in nature is man-shaped and green? Nothing other than a man in green clothes. Remember the Observation chapter? There we pointed out that shape is one of the ways in which objects are seen and perceived.

No, we're not (necessarily) playing soldier, we're being smart. A lot of guys will argue that they are "gray man", but gray man is an impossibility in a WROL situation, because every person moving will be noticed.

Denim is the worst possible choice for preparedness. Jeans are restrictive for movement when they are dry, and they're impossible to move in at all when they are wet. They stay wet forever. Also, blue denim is not a color found in nature.

A compromise you can make is to wear a camouflage top with a pair of outdoor pants in an earth tone, but the ideal really is camouflage.

Avoid commercial camouflage patterns designed for hunting. They are designed to defeat the eyesight of game animals or are really just gimmicks. There is exactly zero risk of game animals shooting back or ambushing you with gunfire. Do I own some? Sure. But would I wear it in a potential life-threatening encounter with violent humans? Absolutely not.

Militaries around the world spend millions and millions of dollars researching how to camouflage personnel and vehicles from human observation, so take advantage of that. Military patterns are also made with insect repellent embedded in the clothing and is also designed to shield you from night vision and IR viewing. Take every advantage that is available. Camouflage clothing that meets military standards gives you the best advantage.

No book or manual can tell you what the best pattern is for your area, and there is no "universal pattern". The US Army experimented with the ACU as a universal pattern, and they found that it didn't really work in ANY environment well.

The next attempt at a universal pattern was Multi-Cam or Multi-Terrain Pattern for the British Forces. Many in the preparedness business swear by it, and call it universal, but it isn't. Even the US and British forces have now come up with temperate, arid, and tropical versions of them. For the record, the British MTP patterns are slightly better than the US Multi-Cam, because they also vary the texture and shapes.

You need to study your terrain and decide what military pattern works best in each season and environment that you are likely to encounter.

As an example, here in Michigan, most people would normally think that desert patterns would never be used, but when you look at Michigan's terrain from late fall through early spring, you'll see lots of dead grass and vegetation in tans and browns that British Desert DPM and USMC Desert MARPAT work perfectly with. As you get farther north, desert pants with a USMC MARPAT top in woodland makes you invisible because of the dead vegetation below your waist and the evergreen trees above your waist.

The point is to analyze your terrain and seasonal changes and decide on what your team should wear. For rapid identification under stress, all wearing the same gear could help.

Review your state laws before deciding as well. The reason is, in some states, like here in Michigan, there are laws that say you cannot wear any part of a US Army or Naval uniform. Now, it's an old law, because it doesn't include the Air Force, but the new Progressive Attorney General in Michigan has vowed to charge militia members under it. A way around this is remove all patches and insignia that specify US Army, US Marines, US Navy, etc.

When considering what camouflage to wear at night, understand that all do not perform equally in the dark. Lighter patterns gather light at night, making them look brighter than the surrounding terrain. I suggest wearing either darker camouflage patterns, or a camouflage specifically designed for night, like midnight digital or Multi-Cam black.

Resist the temptation to wear all black at night. Nighttime is rarely black. Wearing all black makes you stand out at night by being darker in color than your surroundings.

In an urban environment, the best camouflage is just looking like everyone else, which we will discuss in our chapter on Gray Man Tactics.

However, things may be so bad in an urban environment that you are only moving at night or you want a more militant posture to discourage attacks. In that case, for daytime use, most desert patterns are better in an urban environment than woodland types. You could also use urban specific patterns, as long as it's something REALLY used by either law enforcement or military, like Multi-Cam Black or ATACS LE. There are many "urban camo" patterns (like urban digital) that are just a gimmick with no real science behind them.

At this point, you're probably thinking, "Man, I need like 4 different patterns". Yes, if you truly want to be camouflaged, it takes more than throwing on your Ultra Tacti-Cool Multi-Cam OCP combat shirt. There is a lot of thought that goes into this and remember, for the most part, we are talking about avoiding being seen. As an aside, if you are in that hypothetical role of resisting a tyrannical government or a Chinese invasion, camouflage clothing becomes MORE important, not less.

I want to include a short note about the current trend in the tactical world of putting on a camouflage shirt and rolling the cuffs up to mid-forearm. That's fine ON THE RANGE. If you are in a real-world situation, you need the sleeves rolled down. You are losing the camouflage and IR resistance capabilities, as well as insect repellent quality. In a WROL situation, an insect bite or a scrape from a branch can become fatal. Sorry, Ultra Tacti-Cool guys, the sleeves stay down. When you see "Special Ops" guys doing this on TV or in movies, what you aren't seeing is that they wear aviator gloves that go higher than normal gloves during operations, so the skin is still covered.

When you decide on camouflage patterns that will work for you, in your environment, in all your seasons, remember that there are accessories that you need, like a field jacket in the same pattern, or a lightweight jacket. Hats should also be in that same pattern. For each pattern I own, I have a baseball/patrol cap and a Boonie hat in the same pattern. The patrol cap can be worn while moving (it's not as hot), and I can switch to the Boonie when in a static position or higher risk situation.

A Boonie hat is important for a couple of reasons. First, it keeps the sun off your face and neck, which will be helpful with no drugstores selling aloe vera gel. Second, it breaks up the familiar outline of the human head. Third, as long as you buy a high quality one, it has loops for attaching local foliage to the hat to better break up the outline of the head.

As a final note on clothing, also consider footwear. Back in ancient history, the USMC issued us all black combat boots, and we had to keep them highly shined. You may have noticed that they don't anymore. That's because shiny black things don't exist in nature. Get boots that are rough textured, like current issue boots, and in a brown or tan color, just like the US and British military are currently issuing. It's more natural looking and will blend in better. I do still have a black pair for urban or night use, however.

Individual Camouflage

Let's discuss face paint. There isn't a secret to this, and all those discussions about splotch patterns or striped patterns is unnecessary. There are a few rules, but don't worry about trying to make a masterpiece, just make your face look like anything other than a human face.

For those who say "Only white faces need camouflage paint"; that is nonsense. A black or brown face still looks like a face. You still need to camouflage it.

Here are a couple of rules:

1. Darken shine areas like the forehead, your nose, your ears, and your chin.

2. Lighten darker areas like under the nose and chin, and around the eyes.

3. Don't forget the back of the neck, the back of the ears and the backs of your hands.

When selecting camouflage paint, you can get either military issue or commercial, but make sure that it is odorless. The military issue paint is also insect repellent and IR resistant. Commercial styles and some military ones come with a mirror, which you can use while applying it.

After applying face paint, understand that it may need to be re-applied due to sweat. It can also come off if you rub your face frequently.

A lot of "experts" say you don't face paint if you're going to wear a mask or neck gaiter, but they are wrong. Even in a mask, the area around your eyes is exposed and at some point, you will want to take a drink or eat. Face masks and neck gaiters are a supplement to individual personal camouflage, not a replacement.

Additionally, do you really think that after mile 6 on an August afternoon, climbing hills all day, you're going to be motivated to wear a layer of cloth over your face? My personal gear set is a neck gaiter or full mask worn around my neck while moving. If I get in a static position, or if contact is probable, I'll pull up the mask/neck gaiter.

The same goes with gloves. Yes, there are camouflage or OD gloves everywhere. But, at some point, I'm probably taking the gloves off. I generally only wear ultra-lightweight camouflage liner gloves while moving, but in a WROL situation, I'd have camouflage paint on the backs of my hands, too.

For those who wonder why twice I've said only the backs of your hands: Because the front of your hands will sweat it off almost instantly and you may want the front of your hands for signaling other team members. The paint is also greasy and would make weapon manipulation difficult.

<u>Camouflaging Your Gear</u>

By now, if you've read the Base Line Training Manual, you should have a camouflage patterned backpack or rucksack, because Gray Man goes out the window as soon as the WROL situation hits. I understand, though, that some may have purchased an expensive backpack and may not have the funds to buy a new, quality one in camouflage.

The best way to camouflage a backpack that isn't already in a camouflage pattern is to buy a pack cover. They are elastic fitted and come in various sizes and are generally waterproof. You can put the cover on your bag, and you now have a camouflage backpack. This is important for overall safety as well as for when we need to stash our backpack temporarily. There are even some that are reversible, with different patterns on both sides.

You can also run a pair of bungee cords around your patrol pack or ruck, so that you can attach local vegetation to the pack, camouflaging it. Another idea is tying strips of burlap to the MOLLE webbing.

When you need to stash your bag, make sure it's a spot you'll remember. Good spots are under downed logs, under dense underbrush, or at the base of evergreen trees with low hanging branches. Cover it with either downed branches or local foliage and it's invisible for later pickup.

I know, it seems counter-intuitive to hide a bag full of life-saving supplies, but I assure you, there won't people out just looking for hidden backpacks. It will be fine if it is temporary and well-hidden. We shouldn't be stashing a backpack for more than a couple of hours.

When in an individual position, like a fighting position, overnight site, or an observation post, it should be sitting next to you, with a handle pointed towards you, so that you can grab it and run if you need to. If in the kneeling position, it stays on your back, in the prone it should be lying next to you on your support side.

This is why at least a carry handle on top is vital. You can then carry it without having to put it on, if you must leave immediately, or if you need to move just a short distance. I have a couple that also have carry handles on the side.

If you want to camouflage your personal defense weapon, whether it be a long gun, pistol, or both, you can paint them or have them professionally coated. You can also tie strips of cloth to the gun, just ensure that it won't interfere with the gun's operation or sights. There also conforming wraps or tapes specifically for applying camouflage to firearms.

Another idea for camouflaging weapons is to attach rubber bands to the weapon, and place handfuls of vegetation in the rubber bands. Just remember to change it out as it wilts.

Your Belt Kit/web gear (782 gear to us old Marines) should already be in an earth tone or appropriate camouflage pattern.

Radio antennas are camouflaged by hiding them in trees, wherever possible.

Camouflaging Positions

Whether it's your over-night site, an observation post, or a perimeter security position, having the ability to camouflage a position is absolutely necessary.

Having said that, it's important not to over-camouflage. If one area looks like a massive pile of vegetation, and the area around it doesn't, it will still draw attention. Walk out and view it from the front and make changes to either better hide it or make it look less obvious. Check this regularly and replace witling camouflage.

Here, we will give a few pointers. In the section on individual positions, there will be more specific tips applicable to each type of position.

First, let's consider camouflage from ground level observation. Place your position where there is a background that it can blend in with.

If it's a tent, you'll have to place camouflage leaned on the tent or place objects around it to break up its appearance. That's where having an earth toned tent helps significantly. Another idea is to run a strand of para-cord just above the tent and place a camouflage tarp in an A-Frame over the tent. Not only will this help hide it from ground observation, but it also covers you from overhead observation and helps with keeping rain or snow out.

Fighting positions and observation posts should be dug into the ground (see the Individual & Team Position). Camouflage them by placing foliage along the edges, breaking up the straight-line appearance.

For overheard observation, you can place a camouflage tarp over the top. Another idea is building a lean-to type of structure over the top of a ground-level position, using natural materials like logs and the dirt from the hole you dug. After placing the logs, cover them with a tarp or poncho, and then put grass or other foliage on top of it. It's now camouflaged and waterproof.

Another point to consider regarding overhead observation is the bottom of any holes you have dug. It will appear as a square or rectangle from above. Place grass or foliage in the bottom of the hole to prevent mud, and to camouflage the hole from overhead.

The reason we must worry about overhead observation in a WROL situation is the prevalence of drones. If someone can charge them, they can be used. Drones generally also transmit images back to the controller either by radio, WIFI, or by storing images to be reviewed when the drone returns. Additionally, if we are in the hypothetical "resisting a Chinese invasion/tyrannical government" alternate universe, they will have drones and helicopters.

A final camouflage consideration is from thermal observation. Using a survival tarp that is heat reflecting on one side and camouflage on the other to cover you position will shield your heat signature. You could also sleep under one.

Camouflaging Vehicles

The only thing we can do with vehicles, aside from hiding them inside buildings or caves, is to park them under overhead cover like trees, and covering them with either a camouflage net or a camouflage tarp.

Focus on covering reflective surfaces like windows and breaking up the outline.

Training Standard

- Be able to discuss the factors to consider in selecting a camouflage pattern for your environment.

- Demonstrate the ability to camouflage yourself including headgear and face paint.

- Demonstrate how to camouflage a backpack/rucksack that must be dropped temporarily.

- Demonstrate how to camouflage an individual position, including a tent and a fighting position/Observation Post.

- Be able to explain overhead observation concerns.

- Be able to explain how to camouflage a vehicle.

Tactical Wisdom

Fieldcraft

Chapter 10

Field Positions

*I will stand my watch
and station myself on the ramparts.*

Habakkuk 2:1a

In a WROL situation, we won't have police patrols, alarm companies, or email alert chains to warn us of approaching danger. We also won't be able to just call 911 and wait for help to arrive. If a threat emerges, we will have to station ourselves on the ramparts to protect our property or crops.

In order to prevent surprise, we will also have to stand our watches in observation posts, watching critical road junctions or avenues of approach to detect trouble from as far away as possible.

In this chapter we discuss how to site, build, and camouflage individual and team fighting positions and observation posts, as well as how to properly operate from them.

You might be thinking, "I won't need that", but you will. There will no police coming and if you are either growing your own food or living off a food supply you've prepared, there will eventually be people wandering along who will wonder if they can take what you have. Having a prepared defense and appearing ready to defend it may convince them to go elsewhere. If not, you'll be at a significant advantage over your attackers.

Some of the arguments I get on this are "But I'm so far out in the country & that looting stuff will be in the cities". That's true, right up until the cities are picked clean. Then, hungry people will venture out, and consider doing bad things they've never considered doing before, due to desperation.

No matter how remote your location is, you should at least be prepared to mount a defense, and, as we say in the Marine Corps, "Prepare to repel boarders". Having a solid defensive plan and paying attention to who is moving around your location is vital, when there are no police patrols to do it for you. Even in rural areas, you essentially pay the sheriff to patrol for bad elements. You won't have him in a WROL situation.

<u>Individual Positions</u>

The most basic position is called a "scrape" in the US Marine Corps and a "Ranger Grave" in the US Army. It's essentially any small terrain feature that puts your body just below the ground surface if you were prone in it. It can be either a small depression, or a quick "scrape" that you make with your shovel/entrenching tool. Make sure, though, that if you intend to sleep in it, to cut it a little deeper where your hips will sit for comfort.

An individual fighting position is much more complex but should be built anywhere that you intend to defend, such as a long-term camp or a bug out location. Urban fighting positions will be discussed in the Basic Urban Skills chapter.

This position is intended for one defender. Begin by digging a hole as deep as you are tall and wide enough to allow just a little movement. Save the topsoil for camouflaging the hole. Pile the dirt around the hole in a parapet, about 3 feet wide (to stop bullets) and about 6 inches tall. Leave about 6 inches from the edge of the hole to the parapet as an elbow rest or a place to rest optics on a small tripod.

At the bottom of the hole, leave the front side slightly shorter than the back, allowing you to have a "fire step" to stand on to fire out of the hole, and allow you to step down in the back portion and be under the ground surface for cover. This step also allows you to sit on the step to rest.

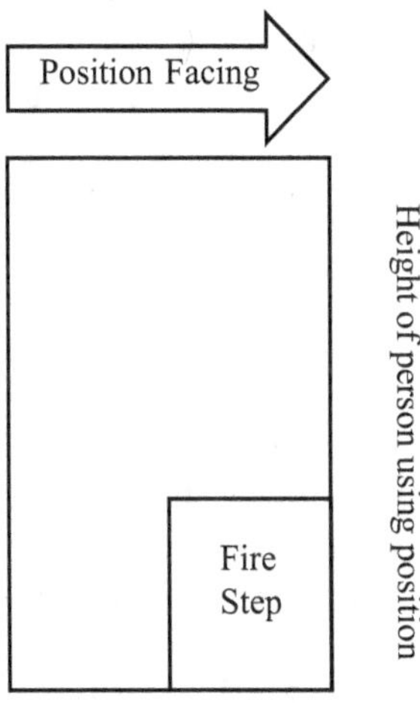

To make a two-person position, simply expand the length to accommodate two people.

Camouflage the position by first placing the topsoil with the grass/ground cover on the front side of the parapet to hide the raw earth appearance of the dirt. Then, use natural materials to break up the positions outline, without limiting its ability to see and engage to the front. Don't over-camouflage the position.

Construct overheard cover using logs. You can either use dirt from the hole to make a support to hold up the logs, or you can build some type of lean-to. You could also just build a lean-to with a camouflage tarp over the position but covered with natural cover.

Observation Posts

Observation posts are built in much the same way, but how they are sited becomes more important, as does camouflage. The purpose of an observation post (OP) is to watch a selected avenue of approach and allow for some early warning back to the rest of your team.

When selecting a site for an OP there are a few key considerations:

1. There needs to be a covered and concealed route from the main perimeter to OP.

2. The OP needs to be able to be secured by the main perimeter positions. In other words, it needs to be close enough that personnel inside your perimeter can providing covering fire for people in the OP.

3. It shouldn't be placed in obvious places like the proverbial church tower or the top of a high hill.

4. When using a hill for an OP, don't put it on top, place it part way down, so that it isn't silhouetted by the sky.

5. The OP should be able to maintain radio communications with the main perimeter. Consider how you can camouflage any external antennas that you use (such as in a tree).

The OP should be no more than 300 meters (333 yards) from your main positions, and much closer in close terrain.

Remember that an OP is only for observation. It must be able to defend itself if surprised, but the proper response is for the OP team to withdraw after giving the alarm, using stealth and their concealed route back to the perimeter.

It's important for them not to deviate from the planned concealed route back for safety reasons. Consider this…You've just been alerted that a potentially hostile group is approaching your perimeter and two armed people in camouflage appear in your sector, away from the planned route out of the OP. What is your first instinct? Do not stray from the planned route.

In a WROL situation, we don't want to give away our OP locations. If we fought from it and drove off the looters (or those hypothetical Chinese/tyrannical troops), on their next approach, they'll avoid the OP, since they now know exactly where it is.

OPs should be manned by at least 2 people, and they should switch roles every 30 minutes. One is observing through optics (binoculars, spotting scope, or night vision) and the other is providing local security.

Notice I didn't mention sleep. There is NO sleeping in an OP. Switch off teams in the OP to manage sleep, rather than letting people sleep in the OP. The OP is a FORWARD position, outside the wire.

<u>**Overhead Concealment**</u>

The prevalence of drones should make us always worry about being concealed from overhead observation.

Siting positions under tree cover is often enough. Building the overhead cover discussed above will also help and will also help in shielding from thermal and IR viewing. Thermal blankets and traps are also a great tool for overhead concealment, as long as you find one that isn't in high-visibility silver or orange. I found camouflage ones available online.

<u>**Field Fortifications**</u>

If you've got a series of individual positions along your perimeter and it's a permanent or semi-permanent location, such as either a bug out location or your temporary emergency location (a bug out location near your bug out/bug in location in case you need to go wait out a larger force), you should develop the individual positions into a field fortification. This means interconnect them and make them into an integrated defense system.

The first step to this is to develop "rat-lines" or single paths between positions, ensuring that they are concealed from the front, and preferably that they offer cover as well. Using dead ground helps.

Once we've established the lines, we turn them into communication trenches. These are shallow trenches that would allow a person to crawl unobserved from one position to the next. In a semi-permanent position, that's all we need.

In a permanent location, like positions to defend our crop growing fields or compound (usually the same place), we then dig out the communication trenches to full-depth trenches between the positions. This would allow you to move reinforcements and supplies between positions in relative safety in the event of a protracted situation. You would also be able to move wounded people safely out of the positions.

In later volumes, we will discuss adding obstacles into the plan, but for now, site positions and trenches to take advantage of natural obstacles.

Planning the Defense

Any time that you create a defensive position or perimeter, you should immediately begin planning how you would defend it. The most basic way to plan is with sketches.

Many with military experience will know that a "Standard Range Card" is nothing more than a sketch of what the position can see and a plan to defend it. That's all we're doing here.

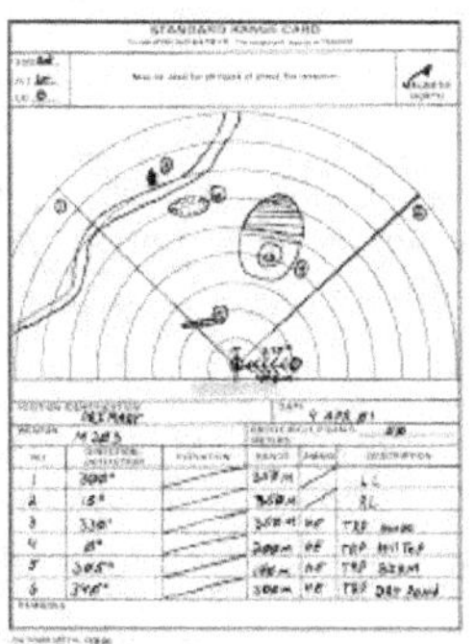

US Army Range Card

Essentially, take any paper and draw the major features that you can see from your position on the range card. Then, either measure or estimate the range to each object. This will help you later when you need to know what adjustments to make on your firearms to engage a target or in describing where you saw something.

Mark danger areas like dead ground on the sketch. In the example above, you'll notice that the sketch has the back of the hill covered in lines; that signifies dead ground because from the position, you cannot see anyone who might be on the back side (reverse slope) of the hill.

Your sketch should also include a North arrow to help in describing directions and where things are.

It's worth noting that in a non-WROL situation, range cards can also help you in your hunting blind, as far as range settings.

Each position should have a range card like this. Rite in the Rain makes them in a foldable-index-card style that is great for field use. They also make some that fit in their binders.

After each position has made a range card, first collect them to create a larger sketch of the entire sector from the individual position cards, then make sure that the range card stays in the position, so that anyone who uses that position can use the card for quick reference. In building your overall sector sketch, you may want to give identifiable features a target designation that will appear on all range cards, so that you can simply call that out on the radio, rather than describing it (Target 4 is quicker to say than the red shed on the northern most hillside). Also, if anyone is listening in on your communications, they won't know where you are talking about.

Remember in the Base Line Training Manual when I said that paper is an overlooked preparedness supply? This is an example.

If you don't have them on Rite in the Rain waterproof paper, you can seal them in sheet protectors or Zip Lock bags.

Another use for paper is that each position, and especially any OPs, need to maintain an "Observation Log". This is nothing more than writing down anything observed in the location. Remember, something small might not warrant a response today, but three weeks later after reviewing various logs, you might detect a pattern that warrants further investigation. Logs should contain the date and time and specific details (including map coordinates) of every observation.

For example, your OP reports that each Tuesday, around 1:30 PM, a guy walks across the frontage of your position. He may not be approaching, but you may want to set up another OP further along his route to see where he's going or coming from, or you may want to send a patrol to stop and chat with him somewhere well away from your OP to see what he's doing.

You will need to write things down for future analysis. Also, in the event that Rule of Law is restored and the wife of the former leader of the local Leroy Jenkins gang tells the sheriff that he was last seen with his boys heading over to your place, you will be able to create a written record of what happened. (Or not, your choice…)

Recap

The individual position, the observation post, and making field fortifications are the basic building blocks of the defense. Remember that in a WROL situation, with very few exceptions, we are on the defense, so we should focus our training, efforts, and time towards the ability to first prepare a solid defense.

We have no business tracking down the Leroy Jenkins Looter crew unless we can first defend our own position from them.

Keeping watch will be a regular part (the bulk of) of life in a WROL situation. These positions, range cards, and observation logs will make that job easier.

Training Standard

- Be able to build an individual defensive position.

- Demonstrate how to effectively prepare a range card for an individual defensive position.

- Explain the concepts for siting an OP.

- Describe field fortifications.

- Explain the purpose and be able to complete an observation log.

Tactical Wisdom

Fieldcraft

Chapter 11

The Gray Man

*...To those not having the law,
I became like one not having the law...*

1 Corinthians 9:21a

I hesitated to include this chapter because so many have a misconception on what Gray Man Tactics are and their role in a post-event WROL society. I decided to include it and thoroughly explain what it means and when you should use it.

Gray Man Tactics are steps we take to make ourselves completely anonymous and non-descript to the casual observer. The best way to describe it is to make yourself completely unremarkable in every way.

I've taught Gray Man tactics to many local groups and organizations, and it amazes me how people show up dressed for a course on Gray Man tactics. The standard is people showing in their tactical pants and some type of tactical polo or field shirt. Just because it's not camouflage, doesn't mean it's Gray Man.

Before I get into what Gray Man tactics are and how to employ them, I want to make something perfectly clear. In a WROL, post-event, societal collapse environment, there is NO Gray Man.

Many people have built their entire preparations and personal security plan around the "Gray Man" concept, but it's just not viable post-WROL. Consider that in a situation when law and order has completely broken down and people are out scavenging for food, any person moving indicates the potential for food and no amount of "blending in" will help. None.

It's far preferable to never be seen at all by operating exclusively at night or in bad weather in some type of night/law enforcement type camouflage pattern and avoiding all contact. We will discuss these tactics in the Basic Urban Skills chapter.

Contrary to popular belief, Gray Man tactics is not a lifestyle. You cannot live your life as a "Gray Man". You have to live somewhere, you have to work, and you have to interact with people at work. Gray Man tactics are things we employ when conducting a particular task or objective, like reconnaissance or information gathering.

For use as a preparedness person or use in any potential "civil conflict", we would most often employ Gray Man tactics and elementary "tradecraft" when out gathering information and intelligence. Tradecraft is the collection of skills that surveillance operatives and intelligence agents use to ply their trade.

When we are in an intelligence gathering mode, we would use Gray Man tactics.

<u>**General Concepts**</u>

There is no single set of clothing or gear that will make you a Gray Man everywhere, so you need to be versatile. If you began your day in a business environment, then business dress or business casual would be the way to start, but if you transition to a neighborhood, you are no longer non-descript, a guy in a suit jacket stands out. The same happens if you began in a casual retail setting and ended up slipping into a high-end clothing store, your jeans and hoodie make you stand out. Versatility is key.

How do we start then? We begin with surveying the area of operations for the day. That's right, you can't just adopt the lifestyle, throw on the 5.11 clothing, and it be good enough. You must put in a lot of work every single day. By the way, 5.11 gear, even the "off duty" shirts, is NOT Gray Man.

Analyze what the plan of the day is. For example, I spent the summer of 2020 undercover inside ANTIFA/BLM protests every single day, wearing a body camera. So, to gather information, I looked at what everyone was wearing at these events. Simple, generally a dark colored hoodie and jeans would be fine.

Conversely, if I wanted to conduct an advance survey of a location like an upscale hotel, then the day calls for whatever everyone else will be wearing in that setting, most likely a suit or sport coat.

So, prior to going to any area on a specific task or mission, determine ahead of time what everyone is wearing in that environment and plan to match that.

The only good factor for COVID-19 was that it made surveillance and Gray Man tactics easy. All you had to do was wear a gray hoodie, jeans, tennis shoes, a baseball cap, and a mask and you were completely anonymous. My point in bringing this up is that rather than vehemently resisting mask mandates, if you want to be a Gray Man, embrace them. I have dozens of solid color face masks that can be swapped instantly.

For general daily use of the tactics, leave the tacti-cool pants and shirts at home. I know, I wear them all the time because they are comfortable and practical, but from a Gray Man standpoint, it marks you out to criminals and law enforcement as someone likely to be armed. That can be either good or bad, but from a Gray Man standpoint, it's disastrous because it singles us out and puts us firmly in one box or another.

For most western nations, like North America and Europe, blue jeans and a grey hoodie are the most anonymous wear. In the summer, a polo shirt can replace the hoodie, as long as it's not a "tacti-cool" polo or in a bright pattern. Pay close attention to any logos on your shirts. Firearms or military logos mark you as unusual, but college logos are anonymous.

The most overlooked aspect of Gray Man tactics is footwear. A guy in jeans and a hoodie, but in his Merrell tactical boots stands out. What do most people in your area wear? If it's the western world, it's some type of athletic shoe. In Mexico, you'd stand out in most areas if you weren't wearing cowboy boots.

The same goes for hats. In most of North America, baseball caps are common, but in Mexico, cowboy hats are more common.

Again, it comes down to studying what is the most common type of wear in any given area and adapting yourself to that.

My personal recommendation is that whatever shirt you decide to wear, you should wear a solid color T-shirt with something on it, like a logo, underneath it. This way, in an emergency, you can quickly change your profile by taking off the top layer. If the opposition are looking for someone in a college hoodie, but you are wearing a shirt with a resort name on it, they will automatically skip over you.

To facilitate Gray Man tactics, you need some type of backpack. Backpacks have become incredibly common and the most common color in North America is black. Don't worry if it has MOLLE webbing on it, because now nearly all backpacks have some variation of it. Just go with solid black.

The reason you need a backpack is because you need to carry a couple of other items to facilitate changing your profile, should it become necessary. In our Gray Man backpack we need:

1. A different top layer - either a polo shirt or hoodie to swap out with the one we had on to enable use to appear as a completely different person.

2. A baseball cap - even if you are wearing one already, having a second one completely different enables another quick change. My rule of thumb is one plain, solid-colored one and one with a team logo in a different color. Completely different appearance.

3. Packable Jacket – They make jackets that fold up very small into their own pocket. Quickly pulling one out and tossing it on is another profile change.

4. Plain black shemagh or bandana – There are a number of ways to wear these that can alter your appearance. If you live in an area with a large Middle Eastern population (mine is majority Middle Eastern), a shemagh is a very

common garment for both men and women. For women, covering their hair to appear Muslim is a great profile change.

5. Folding duffel bag – a serious profile change would be to pull out a different color folding duffel bag and put your backpack inside it after changing your shirt and hat.

6. Flip Flops/Sandals – Despite my general aversion to these, the one thing that law enforcement teaches its people to key in on is footwear, because people rarely change their shoes. Having a pair of flip flops, while not very tactical, can enable you to present a completely different appearance. Understand that the casual observer won't look at your shoes, but law enforcement does, and some cultures look at shoes and handbags first.

In addition to those items, mine has a bulletproof panel (I switch it between bags), a first aid kit, observation devices (monocular), and paper. A good idea is to have a laptop that you can pull out and sit down with. That's a far more common sight in our society than you might imagine. If your laptop/tablet has a forward-facing camera, you can literally sit and videotape people without detection.

I generally clip a small body camera on the strap of my backpack. It looks forward filming what I see and since it is also black, it blends into the strap. I also frequently have a pen camera available.

Ladies, this is not the time for that one-in-a-kind handbag. Stick with the backpack, many women do.

Cover & Cover for Action

In this context, cover means things that shields you from observation. Standing against a pillar can block a camera angle or positioning yourself to the side of a window can prevent you from being seen or being seen completely. Cover is anything that limits someone from getting a good picture or mental picture of you.

Cover for action is a plausible reason for being somewhere. Let's say we are watching a protest and filming people. Just standing there filming makes them notice you. Appearing to be a maintenance person in a yellow vest gives you a reason to be there, cover for action.

Another example comes from the surveillance world. A person sitting behind the wheel of a car watching the front of a building screams "SURVEILLANCE GUY", but a person sitting in the PASSENGER seat doing the same thing says, "that person is waiting for the driver to come out." Simple little things to make your presence less noticeable.

Mannerisms & Movement

Here's where a lot of people go wrong. We want to avoid giving off mannerisms, not try to portray ones that we don't really have. If you don't smoke, don't try to. If you don't write left-handed, don't try to.

Many people try to alter their gait or fake a limp. Rather than blending in, this makes you stand out because you look like someone trying to alter their gait or fake a limp – drawing attention, rather than avoiding it.

An important point is to never run. Even if you think someone is following you, walk. You might want to walk briskly, but always walk. Running draws attention. You might think you are out of sight of whoever you were avoiding, but a random security person seeing you break into a run on camera may decide to investigate…not very Gray Man.

Once, while inside a hostile BLM/ANTIFA crowd, I heard them via radio giving my description and sending three armed men to follow me. If I had broken into a run, they would have known that I was their opposition, and been more determined to pursue. Instead, I walked casually into the deepest part of the crowd, worked my way to the edge, and walked slowly into a parking ramp. Once in there, listening to them trying to figure out where I went, I used the cover and time to change hats, shirt, mask, and take off the sunglasses. Then I emerged from a different exit from the ramp, cut behind a church to my car, and switched backpacks.

I heard them on the radio discussing it, and they agreed that since I didn't run, and was last seen walking closer to the security people, they must have been wrong in identifying me as a potential threat.

I left doubt in their minds by not acting like a fugitive. That's a key point about mannerisms. People new to surveillance or information gathering tend to stare and make furtive glances. Don't act like you're about to rob people, because that draws attention makes them go to a higher alert status.

Surveillance Detection

A big piece of Gray Man Tactics is surveillance detection.

First, I want to dispel a myth. If a national government-level counterintelligence team decides to conduct surveillance on you,

you most likely will never detect it. If you get to that point, you weren't doing Gray Man very well all along, were you? That's beyond the scope of our manual anyway.

Detecting others watching you is as simple as paying attention to your surroundings. Watching for people who act when you pass is the key to surveillance detection.

In the executive protection business, we know that there are two locations a person can be found on any given day. The first is where they sleep, and the second is where they work. The opportunities to begin a surveillance on you are at those two places, every single day.

If you study those places and conduct the Area Study like we discussed in the Base Line Training Manual, you may have noted areas in which someone may be able to watch you enter or leave those areas. Paying close attention to those areas will help you watch for and detect surveillance.

Just as we mentioned before, watch for people sitting in cars, which is the most common way in which surveillance is detected. If you live in a subdivision or cul-de-sac, watch for vehicles that pull out as you leave the sub or street. Anywhere else, watch for cars that pull out after you pass.

Surveillance Detection Route (SDR)

A surveillance detection route, or SDR, is a planned route designed to identify if you are under surveillance. A Gray Man best practice is to have a few worked into your weekly routine. You don't wait until you think you are being followed to check.

It can be as simple as making four left turns in a row or pulling into a business and then pulling right back out again. Anything that would cause a vehicle doing the exact same thing to stand out. Parking ramps are great for this, because many don't charge your card if you're inside less than 5 minutes. However, don't do this in a manner that makes it obvious what you are doing.

The same thing can be done on foot. I will frequently walk directly away from my car, then make a wide circle around several blocks before returning to my car. Anyone else who takes that same foot route is clearly following me and then I will take other actions to break contact, like I described before.

You can also run an assisted SDR. Have a team of your own sitting on a street, and drive past them. Your team watches for anyone following you. You can do the same on foot.
In the resources section, I list a series of books to assist with surveillance and counter-surveillance actions.

SIGINT for Surveillance Detection

SIGINT or Signals Intelligence involves using radios to listen in on others using radios. You can detect surveillance by having a scanner scan the radio frequency spectrum, listening for traffic near you.

In a current-world scenario, local ANTIFA and BLM groups are using the same radios we buy (Baofeng type) and are talking on FRS/GMRS frequencies to avoid enforcement action. Setting up a handheld unit to scan those frequencies can detect surveillance.

Every time I go to an ANTIFA/BLM event, I first scan for their security operating frequency for the day. It doesn't take long to find; they are very active at counter-surveillance and counterintelligence. Being able to listen in is a great asset. As I mentioned earlier, it helped more than once.

In a WROL situation, your communications team should constantly be scanning those same FRS/GMRS/MURS/CB frequencies to detect anyone using radios near your position. If you detect people watching your camp or your compound and using radios, nothing good is about to happen.

Use radios and SIGINT for more than communication. Your communications team should prepare a "SIGINT Intercept Sheet" (nothing more than the date & time and exactly what they heard) every time they hear an unknown radio transmission to be included in your overall intelligence and security awareness.

Being Gray Online

So many of us are so used to narrating our lives on social media that it's outlandish. Lots of people share every little detail. Here are a few tips to stay "Gray Man" online.

1. Set up "Gray Man" profiles with fake names and burner email accounts to do online research.

2. Use a VPN. Every time.

3. Don't share details of your preparations online. Ever.

4. Don't share your travel plans or tag yourself in locations. If you must, tag only when you leave, but understand that you are creating a record of your presence.

5. Tighten account security to not allow others to tag you at locations or in photos. Increasingly, the FBI, in their

political cases, are using photos of people at training events with guns to imply militia or extremist group membership.

6. Don't send friend or follow requests to known ANTIFA/BLM figures. They have an ACTIVE counterintelligence wing that is VERY GOOD. Monitor, but don't try to be secret squirrel.

7. Under that Signal and Telegram are compromised and not as secure as you think.

8. The most secure method of exchanging information is face to face.

9. Don't make "hypothetical" online statements like "Let ANTIFA come to my house, I'll shoot them". If, God forbid, you ever need to, that post or tweet will be Prosecution Exhibit #1.

10. Understand that Facebook began as a Defense Department project. Everything you create anywhere in social media is a record, even if you think you've deleted it. The NSA "scrapes" social media sites several times a day and saves it.

11. Never answer the meme questions "What's your favorite car" or "What town did you grow up in", etc. This is phishing, those answers can be used to guess your security questions.

12. Never, under any circumstances, engage with people who send you message requests and start talking about altering guns, building bombs, or taking drastic actions. Tell them to never contact you again and BLOCK them. Those are

your federal tax dollars at work. For some reason, the government doesn't like self-sufficient people.

13. Don't respond to internet ads about products that can be made into silencers or auto sears. At least one has been proven to have been run by the ATF and the others ALL end with federal agents showing up at your door.

Gray Man Legal Concepts

We aren't ever doing anything illegal, and I don't advocate taking unconstitutional actions, ever. I do, however, recommend highly being Gray Man in your legal dealings.

What do I mean by that? The Fourth, Fifth, and Sixth amendments along with the decisions in Gideon v Wainwright and Miranda v Arizona apply to EVERYONE.

Never consent to a search and never consent to be interviewed without an attorney. That's the Gray Man way. Demanding that police or federal agents follow the US Constitution isn't illegal and it isn't "uncooperative". Them telling you it's uncooperative or saying "well, you must have something to hide" is COERCIVE. I can have nothing to hide, and still not want police digging through my belongings, just to confirm what I already know (that I'm not doing anything wrong). You never have to prove your innocence.

I've also had a couple of employees, in a situation, give statements to police who were 100% on our side and in agreement that my employees acted in self-defense, only to have a liberal, crusading prosecutor charge them with ridiculous charges to make headlines. None of the charges stuck, but the damage was done.

Demand that they honor your rights and use every Constitutional safeguard available to you.

Burner Phones

I hear a lot of talk about these, and I get a lot of questions about them.

Unless you wear a mask and sunglasses, and gloves, paying cash with money you've never touched at a location you've never been with your other phone, you don't really have a burner phone.

Also, you can buy that phone and a minutes card, but in order to get it actually turned on, under the PATRIOT Act, you have to provide some type of identification to the phone carrier. Then, once it's turned on, you would have to NEVER have both phones on at the same time or in the same place. You aren't getting true "burner" service without breaking the law.

I know, you "heard" that drug dealers and spies do it all the time. Yes, but both of those occupations involve regularly breaking the law. Besides, drug dealers use other people's phones, not burner phones.

Using phone VPN is a better idea. That, coupled with never taking your phone anywhere that you don't want to be tracked to. Understand also that your cell phone is a RADIO, and it's broadcasting your conversation. Cell phones aren't your friend.

You can also put your phone in a Faraday bag or cage but understand that you need to do that long before you arrive at a particular location. The phone will log where it last had a signal and where the signal picked up again. It's prudent to do this in logical places, like a store or mall parking lot, rather than while driving around. It will just look like you went into a business and came back out.

A Gray Man House and Car

Applying these concepts, don't put any stickers or decorations on your car that make it stand out or that imply a political or firearms affiliation. Better yet, don't put any on it at all.

At home, also limit political signage, particularly during periods of civil unrest. You can take the flag down for a few days for safety.

Final Notes

This is a very brief overview of an exhaustive concept and I purposefully didn't go into get much detail, because Gray Man is not really for the post-event world. It's a current world intelligence-gathering and self-protection role.

In the resources section, I list a book series that we use in training executive protection and surveillance personnel on surveillance, surveillance detection, and counter-surveillance, which are all "tradecraft skills" that use Gray Man concepts. The books are well-written and highly detailed. They also cover countering electronic surveillance.

Gray Man is no more than remaining aware to the indicators that you are giving off by your dress, mannerisms, and appearance, and attempting to minimize them in every area of your life.

<u>**Training Standard**</u>

- Be able to describe general Gray Man concepts and planning.

- Describe what goes into a "Gray Man" backpack.

- Explain how to conduct surveillance detection and what a Surveillance Detection Route is.

- Be able to explain online Gray Man concepts.

- List Gray Man Legal Concepts.

- Be able to explain when to use Gray Man tactics and when to use Basic Urban Skills and what the difference is.

<u>**Resources**</u>

1. Books by ACM IV Security Services, Paladin Press
    a. Secrets of Surveillance
    b. Surveillance Countermeasures
    c. Countering Hostile Surveillance

Tactical Wisdom

Fieldcraft

Chapter 12

Basic Urban Skills

...for I see violence and strife in the city.
Day and night they go around it on its walls,
and iniquity and trouble are within it; ruin is in its midst;
oppression and fraud do not depart from its marketplace.

Psalm 55:9b-11

The Ultimate Tactical Handbook isn't far off on its description of urban life, and it will only be worse in a WROL situation. When you have a large group of hungry humans together, where some have food, and many don't, nothing good will result. In a WROL situation, being in an urban environment is the worst-case scenario.

That being said, many people won't be able to get out and many plan to "bug in". First, let me say that without a "neighborhood protection group", you won't survive. Start building that NOW.

There are some fieldcraft skills that we can apply to make ourselves a little safer in an urban environment. Here, we will discuss them.

Before we get started though, let me just say right at the outset that we aren't going to be discussing Close Quarters Battle (CQB) or any of those kinds of "tacti-cool" things. We want to remain grounded in reality, and the reality is that you won't be out seizing objectives; your objective is survival.

It's not from a lack of skill, the US Marine Corps ensured that I am well versed in the topic, and some time at Blackwater's US Training Center in the "Principal Recovery & Extraction" course gave me some advanced skills. They just aren't the focus at this level.

The good news is that the urban environment favors the defense. In other words, it's hard to assault a building in the face of a prepared defense. Fortunately for us, defense is our main goal, and we are on a defensive footing.

In addition to not being practical for small groups, CQB is casualty and supply intensive. A small group with limited supplies is not really able to launch an offensive urban campaign. That doesn't mean we can't spring the occasional ambush or make a raid, in the face of a Chinese/Russian invasion, but that's a topic for another book.

In this chapter, we will be concerned with camouflage, movement, and defense.

Camouflage in the Urban Environment

While the basic concepts are the same, we must shift approaches a bit to effectively camouflage ourselves and our gear in the urban environment.

Woodland camouflage patterns aren't ideal in an urban area, because there aren't a lot of greens to blend in to. In the urban environment, the predominant colors will be shades of tan, brown, and gray. For this reason, desert patterns or patterns with varying shades of gray (law enforcement type) work far better.

For gear, rather than attaching foliage, rubber-banding burlap strips to it works effectively.

Basic Urban Movement

The first concept for urban movement is that night is a far better time for movement than daytime.

The second one is that it is far preferable to keep your movement hidden by moving inside buildings, rather than on the street. When moving inside buildings, make sure that you don't silhouette yourself in any doors or windows. If you can't move inside buildings, walking through back yards and alleys is better than being out on the road.

In a neighborhood, if forced by obstacles to move along a road, it's far safer to walk through yards near the houses or along business fronts rather than being directly on the road. Roads are usually being watched and experience in the Balkans shows that snipers use roads as a killing ground, and they don't really care who they target.

In WROL situations like we saw in the Balkans and again in Georgia in 2008 as well as the Ukraine right now, snipers will shoot anyone and then direct their comrades to the body to loot any supplies. Stay out of the road – don't be a loot drop for anyone else.

Crossing a wall is like we discussed before. Take a quick glance over, then roll over the wall fast and low to deny anyone a chance at a target.

When you come to a corner, it's human nature to peek around the corner from a standing position. Since it's also human nature to look for other humans at eye level, this will get you spotted. Either kneel or lay down flat, and only expose a small part of yourself to glance around a corner from well below eye level.

A common urban technique for dealing with doors and windows is called "pieing". This involves pointing your weapon at the opening and looking in at a small slice, then moving slightly and looking at another slice, and so on, until you've viewed the whole opening. It's far better than just looking in.

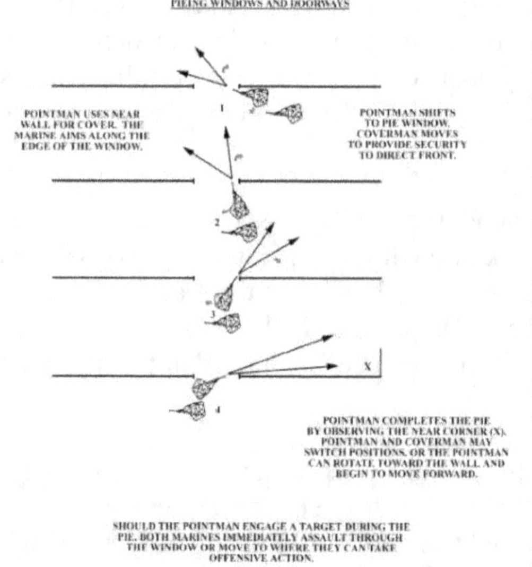

Source: USMC FM 12-10B.1, Military Operations on Urbanized Terrain, 2016

When passing first floor windows, crouch below them and stay as close to the building as possible. You have to pay attention to avoid just walking past basement windows but try to step over them or jump past them, so that you aren't seen or exposed to someone inside.

Movement should always parallel buildings, trying to stay within their shadow as much as possible. Always pick out your next location before moving.

Avoid open areas and roads. If forced to cross a road, cross quickly at the shortest possible distance. We are relying on stealth, not force, so fast and quiet is the rule.

When traversing an urban area, remember that most people will be at ground level. If there is a way to move through or over buildings anywhere above ground level, that's a huge bonus. Consider having a rope and grappling hook to gain access to roofs or enter at higher than ground level.

When forced to enter at ground level, doors are the very last place you want to enter. Look for a hole in the building. If there isn't a hole, enter via a window. A door would be an absolute last resort.

If a group is moving together on the street (or in yards as described above), half of the team moves on one side of the street, and the other half on the far side. That way, each half can watch the upper levels of houses and buildings above the other half. In an urban environment, you must be concerned about the elevated positions more than in a wooded environment.

When moving as a group, rear security becomes vital. In a WROL situation, a group may decide to follow you as you lead them to a food or water stash, then ambush you later.

Intersections are another danger area. Half of your team should secure the near side by taking a knee and watching both ways on the cross street, while the other half crosses and then they set up security on the far side. Then the other half follows.

If the group makes contact with a hostile group, occupy the nearest building and decide what to do. Staying on the street is the worst option. Breaking contact directly away is the best.

Preparing a Building for Defense

A few steps need to be taken to harden a building for defense in an urban area. Make no mistake, if you bug in or occupy a building in an urban environment, someone will eventually come by to see what kind of supplies you have. This is particularly true if everyone else is losing weight from lack of food and you aren't.

Doors that aren't being used should be nailed shut and barricaded. Consider putting plywood over first floor windows and barricading them.

For upper-level windows, attach wire mesh to boards that you can mount over the windows. This will prevent rocks or incendiary devices from being thrown through the windows.

Block off unused rooms and barricade their doors. If you have any unused stairs or hallways, block them with furniture and either razor wire or barbed wire. You can also stage wire to be quickly deployed on stairs or in hallways in the event of an attack.

You need to consider and have an escape plan. Keep in mind that your escape plan should not involve a door or window. Any opposing force that attacks your building will be watching them. In the event of a true WROL situation, cutting a new, concealed opening for emergency use isn't out of the question.

If you live in an apartment building or row house, understand that the basement may run the whole block, as may a crawl-space attic. Those could be escape routes, and entry routes for bad folks as well.

Mouseholes are holes cut in interior walls to allow you to move about without using a hallway. If you are truly preparing your building for defense, consider making them between rooms. You could also make a mousehole in a ceiling to the upper level and use a ladder that you could pull up through the hole, while blocking the stairs completely. This would certainly make sleeping at night more secure.

If you are using FM radio to communicate in your neighborhood or building for security, use the lowest effective power rating. This will keep adversaries from gathering information on guard routines and schedules to plan an attack.

It may seem like we're going over the top with security precautions, but in an urban environment in a post-WROL world, security is your number one concern. People will be out hunting for "easy" targets.

In preparing for defense, we also need to prepare to fight fires. Fire will be a big danger, particularly with no fire department to come to the rescue.

It's an old adage in the preparedness world to fill all tubs and sinks with water, and that helps here. You could also stage buckets of water throughout the structure. It's vital to remember that any water stored for firefighting is only used for that purpose. You don't want to have a fire and have no water. You also don't need to treat or filter firefighting water.

Placing a layer of sand or dirt on the floor could help as well. If
you have fire extinguishers, place them everywhere. While
scavenging buildings for food or firewood, bring back any
unattended fire extinguishers from unoccupied buildings. You can
never have too many.

Some other considerations are making sure that you have adequate
burn first aid treatments available. Fire blankets are also a good
investment.

One of the main causes of fire related injuries is smoke inhalation.
A full respirator mask or military surplus NBC mask can help.

Urban Positions

It's especially important in an urban environment to remember that
you should fire from the ends of obstacles, like walls or vehicles,
rather than over the top.

While we're discussing vehicles, you need to know that they offer
very little cover, despite what you see in the movies. They should
be considered as concealment only. The only real cover is the
engine block and the metal wheels. If you are going to fire from
behind a vehicle, either fire under it from behind the wheels, or fire
through it, never over it.

When using a window, fire from inside the building, making sure
that your muzzle doesn't stick out the window. Use the shadows in
the room as concealment.

A loophole is small firing port made in the side of building to fire
out, rather than using obvious windows. They should be reinforced
with cover (sandbags, etc.) around them. Consider making several
false loopholes, to confuse any opposition.

Roof tops make good firing positions but try to use a chimney or smokestack to break up your outline. A good chimney can also make effective cover.

If you are out in the open and fired on from another building, rather than running away from it, take cover as close to the side of the building they are firing from as possible. For them to fire at you, they would have to lean out a window, enabling you to defend yourself (or another member of your team could take action to defend you).

Consider blocking your road with vehicles with flattened tires (they can't be rolled out of the street by attackers).

Urban Observation Posts

We still need OPs in an urban environment. In fact, they are even more vital.

You can get more creative in an urban setting as well, depending on the situation. If there is relative calm with only sporadic issues, an OP could be as simple as two people sitting on a porch with a hidden radio or someone on a rooftop.

It's harder to detect your OPs in an urban environment if you put them in buildings and they practice noise and light discipline. Stealth is absolutely vital and listening becomes more important.

In an urban environment, it's harder to "tell the sheep from the goats" so pattern analysis and behavior analysis becomes key. Look for people who appear to be "hunting" rather than just looking for food. Predators hunt for victims.

Select as OP locations places with a longer view, like elevated locations or a house on a hill. Avoid water towers and church steeples, as these are obvious and the first place anyone else will look.

Again, stealth and security are vital, because if a bad element sees that you have an OP out, they will wonder what you have that is worth protecting. A great way to insert an OP team covertly is to always use male/female teams. The teams can trade off outer jackets. To anyone watching, it will look like the same couple walked out and then walked back.

Subterranean Operations

There's an entire city underneath every urban area in the industrialized world. Sewer systems, storm water runoff systems, utility tunnels, and subways form a labyrinth underneath your feet. There is an entire network into and out of every urban area, completely underground.

These systems provide outstanding tactical value to anyone who understands how to use them.

First, understand what they do. Yes, one of these systems handles raw sewage and that's our system of last resort. However, a sanitary storm sewer, while not exactly a pleasant babbling brook, is a cleaner system that generally takes rainwater from inside a city and runs it outside the city. With a little pre-planning and recon, you can find a completely hidden way into and out of anywhere.

Safety is paramount. While you obviously wouldn't jump into a storm sewer during a storm, there are other hazards as well. When you first remove a manhole cover, leave it open for 10-15 minutes to let gases that may have built up there dissipate.

Your entire team, while in a sewer system, needs to be tied together with a safety line, in case one person falls.

Respirator or NBC masks can help with filtering gases or odors. While moving underground, if anyone feels lightheaded, immediately open the nearest manhole and exit for fresh air. You should be frequently doing this as you move. You can also open manholes to check street signs to make sure you know where you are.

Whenever you are doing recon in a sewer or subway system, mark with chalk or chem-lights the way you came from to prevent getting permanently lost.

Any tunnel system will be very dark. Blue and red lens flashlights can help or use night vision. There won't be enough light for passive night vision, so you'll have to use active. Understand the security risk that poses in that it is the same as using a white-light flashlight if anyone else is in the tunnel using night vision.

From a defensive standpoint, consider blocking storm sewer access to your neighborhood by filling it with debris. Weigh that against the risk of flooding.

Recap

These are very basic urban fieldcraft skills designed to increase your survivability, should you have to traverse an urban area. I don't recommend bugging in in this environment, but I understand that some of you have no choice. These skills should help.

Anytime you are in an urban area (even now), you should have at least two plans for getting out, one in a vehicle and one on foot.

Even if you are bugging in, you need an emergency bug-out plan. Remember, once you are fully into a WROL situation, the Gray Man goes out the window. You need to present a strong and militant position to discourage anyone who is emboldened by the lack of police. A Gray Man posture would actually invite attack, rather than reduce the risk, like it does pre-WROL. Do not confuse the two situations.

Training Standard

- Describe urban camouflage principles.

- Explain how to select routes in urban terrain.

- Demonstrate the proper method for looking around corners.

- Demonstrate "Pieing" openings.

- Demonstrate crossing an intersection as a member of a team.

- Explain how to harden a building.

- Describe firefighting preparations.

- Explain various urban firing positions.

- Describe the safety rules for subterranean operations.

Tactical Wisdom

Fieldcraft

Chapter 13

Land Navigation

Ponder the path of your feet;
then all your ways will be sure…

Proverbs 4:26

Land navigation is the critical skill of being able to find your way from one point to another, using a map and compass, or natural signs, to guide way. It's essentially the ability to get somewhere. As the piece of Tactical Wisdom above says, ponder your path and your ways will be sure.

When we talk about land navigation, a lot of people say, "Well, I have a $600 GPS, so I'm good". There's a problem with that in that it relies on technology. At the beginning of this series, we said that our strategies need to be no-to-low tech.

Aside from the issue of finding batteries or an EMP strike zapping your $600 unit, there are other inherent issues in relying on GPS. The first is that the GPS system is owned & managed by the US Department of Defense. Before you start saying "but, GLONASS", GLONASS is owned and operated by the Russian Ministry of Defense.

What does this mean for preparedness? During the Second Amendment Rally in Richmond, Virginia in January 2020, participants noted that they could not receive GPS signals around Richmond. Later, the US Navy announced that a carrier task force had conducted an exercise off the Virginia Coast that involved jamming and denying access to the GPS system. I'm sure it was just a coincidence.

This isn't solved by switching to a GLONASS receiver, either. Currently, with tensions high on the Ukraine/Russia border, surveillance drones are crashing due to GPS jamming of GLONASS & EU GPS Systems by the Russians.

Relying on GPS, which is a MILITARY system, for use in a WROL situation is not the best alternative. That being said, I have one, but it is a supplement to the map and compass.

Another issue is that the entire US system is managed from a ground station at Schriever Air Force Base outside Colorado Springs. What do you suppose will happen if that location is destroyed? If I know it's there, you can be assured that China & Russia do as well.

Additionally, under Federal law in the US, your GPS receiver is classified technically as "munitions", because it can be used for targeting. That's not by mistake. It keeps you from sending one to your cousin in Turkmenistan, but it also allows the seizure or criminalization of possession of it during a declared emergency under the National Defense Authorization Act.

In Western Society, we've become far too comfortable and over-reliant on technology like phones and GPS. The art of land navigation has been mostly lost. Even advanced military units are tending to over-rely on GPS.

GPS/Online Mapping

Many people still insist on having a unit, and I have one too, so let's discuss what you need and keeping it updated. First, have an outdoor unit, not a car unit.

In selecting a handheld unit, it's best to get one that accepts the uploading of topographical maps. In a WROL situation, I don't care how many McDonald's there on my route, but I do care about hills and water. Mine (an older Magellan Triton I had a software person update and harden), accepts them in SD cards, which is a great feature, because I can transfer the maps to my computer or tablet for marking and updating, and then back to the GPS.

Find a unit that comes with at least annual base map updates. Another good feature is the ability to receive both US WAAS signals and GLONASS.

Buy detailed (24K scale) topographic maps for the unit for any areas you might operate in. I have fully ¼ of the US loaded onto my receiver.

As far as settings, I recommend changing the map coordinates to MGRS or Military Grid Reference System, rather than traditional latitude and longitude. It's far easier to convert those coordinates to a paper map and vice versa.

Cell phone GPS is actually a surveillance tool designed to spy on you disguised as a feature, but many of you swear by it. Whatever mapping service you use on your phone (I use Google), see if it allows an "offline map". This is a map downloaded to your phone, so that you can navigate without a cellular connection. On a daily basis, your phone downloads sections of map as you move from area to area, so if you don't have an offline map stored, without cell service, your phone's GPS receiver is useless. Having an offline map stored directly on your phone will allow you to use the phone as a GPS unit without a signal. Just be sure to put your phone in Airplane Mode, so that it doesn't run down your battery searching for a cell signal. Also, update those maps as often as possible.

A note about cellular GPS service and privacy… You can't really turn it off. It still gathers the data, so plan accordingly. The other thing is that when you first set up a phone, it asks you about using WIFI hotspots and other systems to "improve location accuracy" …that's a LIE. Decline that permission because they are only trying to build a database of what businesses you are nearby for selling targeted ads.

COMPASSES

The most important piece of the land navigation art form is a quality compass. Not just a compass, a quality compass. You will want to spend some money here to get a good one, not a $10 pin on compass.

The bare minimum features are:

- Either luminous or phosphorescent dial, this enables nighttime use.

- Some type of aiming device.

- A rotating bezel for setting courses/night use.

- At least a full degree scale, and a preferable a mil scale as well.

My personal choice is a US issue lensatic compass, made by Cammenga. It's best feature (especially as I get older) is the magnifying lens for reading the azimuth.

Nice to have features are some type of straight-edge with a scale for measuring distances on the map. A lanyard is another plus because a compass is a vital piece of gear. Tie the compass to your belt or web gear.

Some Silva compasses include a "romer" in various compass scales. A romer is tool for reading grid squares on a map (more on that in a moment). A map protractor is a tool with a romer, a degree/mil scale, and plotting tools. You NEED a protractor. Mine, by RM Military, has back azimuths (see below) pre-printed.

Whatever compass you get, spend time learning everything you can about it and how to use that specific type. You will be betting your life on it just as surely as your defensive firearm skills, so invest the time. For example, I know that each click on my rotating bezel moves the luminous mark 3 degrees. Knowing that will allow me, in the dark, to move the mark 30 degrees by making 10 clicks, rather than turning on a flashlight to find a heading of 330 degrees after finding north.

An azimuth is the heading to a particular spot. For example, if I want to know the azimuth I'm moving on, I will pick out an item in front of me, hold my compass steady and level, and point the compass at the object. The number underneath the index line is the azimuth to that object, or the heading I'm going.

A back azimuth is just like it sounds, the heading I'd need to follow if I wanted to turn around and go back in the direction I came. It's useful to know this when following a route, and then returning. On the way out, you'll follow the planned azimuths. On your way back, you'll compute and follow the back azimuths.

To compute a back azimuth, if the current azimuth is more than 180 degrees, subtract 180. If the current azimuth is less than 180 degrees, add 180 to it to get the back azimuth.

Maps

If you've read literally anything I've ever wrote or looked at my blog, you'll know how I feel here. Paper maps are absolutely essential, and you need many. There is no such thing as too many maps.

There is no "one size fits all" mapping solution either. We know that I'm a huge proponent of topographic maps, but inside a dense urban area like Detroit or Minneapolis, there is nothing better than a street map. In farmland, an "Atlas" type hybrid map like we discussed in Chapter 6 is the best. In rural, wild areas, the topographic map is king.

My personal solution is a combination of all three.

As I mentioned in Chapter 6, you can download mapping from the USGS in any scale you need. They come in a default of 1:25,000. For more information, see the Resources Section at the end of Chapter 6.

The map legend contains information on how to read the map and what all the symbols mean.

The key piece of marginal information on the map is the "GM Angle" or declination. The Earth is giant rock, and its magnetic properties are not constant. The magnetic north pole is not directly

on top of the earth. The declination shows you how many degrees
to add or subtract to find true north, also known as Grid North –
"GM Angle" refers to the difference between Grid North (the top
of your map) and Magnetic North.
If you don't adjust for declination or the GM Angle either
mathematically or by adjusting your compass, you will drift off
target. For a short distance, like 500 meters, that's not a big deal.
However, if you move 5 miles, you could be off by half a mile or
more. It multiplies quickly. Some compasses allow you to
manually adjust your compass so that they match, but it's easier to
just remember to make the addition or subtraction.

In most of North America, you will subtract. For example, here in
Michigan, magnetic north is actually not at 360 degrees, but at 354
degrees, a -6° GM Angle/Declination. If I don't adjust for those
degrees to the west, I'll end up walking off to the northwest right
into Lake Michigan.

Before we can navigate using a map, we need to be able to know
where we are. This is called "orienting" the map. If we know what
direction north is, like by using our compass, minus the declination,
we start by turning the map until the top is pointed north.

Now that we have it facing the right way, we need to know exactly
where we are. The process of finding our location is called
resection.

- Locate two terrain features that you can see that are on the
  map.

- Using the compass, determine the azimuth to each object
  and write it down (see why I keep saying paper is a
  preparedness supply?)

- Convert the magnetic azimuths to a grid azimuth by subtracting or adding the GM angle/declination.

- Convert to a back azimuth using the above formula (adding or subtracting 180 degrees).

- Using a map protractor or your compass, draw a straight line on the map from both terrain features on the back azimuth.

- Where the line intersects is where you are standing (magic, right?)

To find the map coordinates of something you see and want to notate, like a potentially hostile camp, or a sighting of another group, we do the exact opposite and it's called finding a location by intersection.

- Once your map is oriented and you know your location, shoot an azimuth to the location you want to find and write it down, adjusting for the GM angle.

- Move to another location and shoot an azimuth to the location again.

- Using your compass or a map protractor, draw lines from the two known locations on the azimuths you wrote down.

- Where the lines cross is the location you want the coordinates of.

- Use the romer to get the coordinates.

Maps, especially topographical maps, are broken down into grid squares, with numerical designations. These can be from the Military Grid Reference System (MGRS), the Universal Transverse Mercator (UTM) Grid, or any other.

To determine the location coordinates on the map, use the romer of the appropriate scale to find the exact coordinates. On a grid map, "eastings" are the vertical lines, running north to south and they are numbered from left to right (going east). "Northings" are the horizontal lines running west-east, and they are numbered from bottom to the top (going north).

Generally, just knowing the easting and northing results in a large area. We define that as a grid square, and it is named according to the lines which meet in the southwest corner. A four-digit grid gives the easting first and the northing second. Depending on the map scale, that can result in a huge area.

To make it more precise, the romer breaks a grid square into tenths for a "6-dgit grid". You place the corner of the romer on the spot you want a coordinate of, and the nearest number where the romer crosses the grid becomes the third number in the easting and northing.

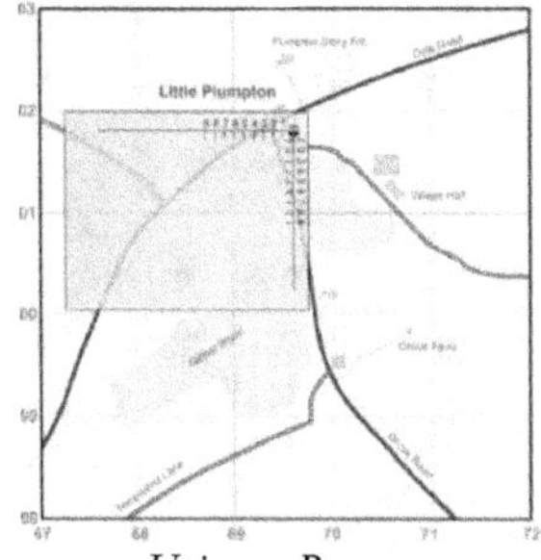

Using a Romer
Source: Wikipedia

Some maps come with 3-digit easting and northing grids. They allow your coordinates to be even more accurate and are called an "8-digit grid".

Earlier, we talked about using the offset method to go around an obstacle. We can use our compass to that, as illustrated in USMC Manual "Scouting & Patrolling":

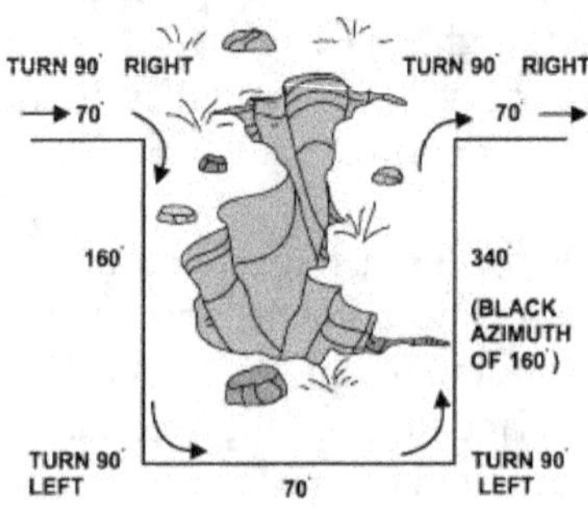

Offset Method
Source: USMC MCTP 3-01A

Handrailing

There is a skill that will enable you to still have a good idea of where you are going, even without a compass and a map. Following roads or terrain features can ensure that you stay on a particular route.

The problem is that these are known militarily as "natural lines of drift", or areas in which humans will be moving. In a WROL situation, other people mean risk. There will be others moving along every road, path, electrical transmission line, river, and railroad.

Let's take rivers as our example. Every major city in the world is on a river. This is because, for all human history, we've been drawn to sources of fresh water, and rivers made a way to conduct trade, as well obtain food and water. Ancient hunting tribes followed rivers because game was drawn to the water as well.

Building on that in a modern setting, people will be drawn to walk away from danger along natural pathways, like rivers, highways, roads, railways, utility cleared corridors, and the like.

In order to avoid encountering other people, the US military trains patrols to do what is known as "handrailing". Handrailing refers to moving along a terrain feature, whether man-made or natural, by always keeping it in sight, while not actually using the feature for movement.

You can follow the path of a highway by remaining in the concealment of woods along the highway, but 100-200 meters to the side. Even in farmland, you'll see ditches or wood-rows traversing the fields, that would allow you to remain safely concealed while moving.

In using highways to handrail, it helps to understand how the interstate highway system operates to help navigate. There are two different systems, the US Highways and US Interstates. The rules are listed here:

- North-South Routes: On US Highways, they are numbered with odd numbers, beginning in the east, and getting higher as you move west. Interstates are also odd numbers, but with the lowest in the west, and the highest in the east.

- East-West Routes: On US Highways, they are numbered with even numbers, beginning in the north, and getting higher as you move south. Interstates are also even numbers, but with the lowest in the south, and the highest in the north.

- Spur Routes: A spur is shorter section off the main highway, with a number in front of the two-digit main route.

As you can see, by knowing these rules and handrailing the highway, you can indeed navigate fairly well.

However, when traveling in more remote areas, you may have to handrail a terrain feature like a river or a railroad (maybe a power line). Avoid the temptation to travel directly along the feature, as you will surely encounter other people, some of whom will have bad intentions or just be very desperate.

When planning routes on a map, you can plan to handrail, using a map and compass to track progress as well.

<u>**Training Standard**</u>

- Describe the risks involved in relying on GPS only.

- List the minimum features needed on a compass.

- Demonstrate how to obtain an azimuth and how to calculate a back azimuth.

- Explain what declination is and how to account for it.

- Locate your position by resection.

- Plot an unknown location by intersection.

- Demonstrate determining grid coordinates using a romer.

- Explain handrailing.

Tactical Wisdom

Fieldcraft

Chapter 14

Team Organization & Movement

*Then you will go on your way in safety,
and your foot will not stumble.*

Proverbs 3:23

Once you've learned individual movement, it's time to start developing the ability of your team to move together. It may seem simple at first, but when we are talking about a WROL environment, where we are trying to avoid being seen or tracked, and the potential for everyone we meet to be armed, it takes on a new level of difficulty. Additionally, we need to be concerned not just with moving from point A to point B, we need to be concerned with doing so in a secure manner.

The first step to this is to organize your team. A lot of your organization will be based on the size of your group. Both the US Army and the US Marine Corps organize into 4 man "fire teams", and that should be your basis. The US Army places 2 fire teams in a squad and the USMC has 3 teams. The difference is because the US Army generally travels in fighting vehicles and US Marines generally travel on foot. The British Army is also organized in 4-person fire teams, with 2 fire teams making a "Rifle Section".

It's up to you how to organize the larger group, but you should use the 4-person fire team model as a basis, since it clearly is effective. Don't worry so much about titling your teams as "fire teams" or "squads", just make sure each person is part of a permanent team. In this way, they'll learn to anticipate how each person in their team will act.

Below the fire team level is the "buddy pair". Each person should have a "buddy" or "partner" with whom they always move or operate. The buddy pair concept originated in the Ultimate Tactical Handbook:

> *Though one may be overpowered,*
> *Two can defend themselves.*
>
> *Ecclesiastes 4:12b*

The buddy pair is the building block of our entire security posture. One provides security while the other sets up their shelter, then they switch. It's the same with every task. When one is watching left, the other watches right. When one moves, the other provides cover.

In the fire team organization, the buddy pairs act as a "buddy pairs" to each other. When one pair moves, the other pair covers. When one pair performs a task, the other pair provides security. This is the entire basis for the fire team organization, security & mutual support.

In this volume, we are going to discuss a couple of very basic foot formations for a team to move with. There are many more, but these basic ones will help a team learn to move and be effective together. They will also allow a team to provide good security all around their formation. Remember, we are talking about movement formations, not combat ones. In later volumes, we will address more advanced formations for more advanced situations, like the entirely hypothetical resistance movement.

Security

In a WROL situation, security is our number one concern. It becomes even more vital anytime we are outside of our base location because there will no longer be consistently functioning law enforcement.

I say, "consistently functioning", because I'm sure that there will be agencies trying to operate and trying to maintain some semblance of order. Those agencies (predominantly County Sheriff's) will mostly be tied up manning checkpoints or securing critical infrastructure, rather than conducting patrols or answering calls for service. They'll be in small towns and city centers, not in the countryside or neighborhoods.

That's why we need to become obsessive about our personal security and collective security.

Whenever a group is moving, the person in front is responsible for security to the front, the person at the rear is responsible for rear security, and those in the middle will be responsible for flank (side) security. That seems easy, but the tendency is to watch the person in front of you while walking, rather than looking outward and watching for threats.

Whenever your group halts, for whatever reason, you will adopt one of two security postures.

- **Short Halt Posture:** Each person takes a knee behind the nearest cover or concealment, watching their sector. Each person alternates the direction they are facing. The person in front faces the front, and the person at the rear faces the rear. Everyone keeps their backpack on. On a short halt, 100% security watch is maintained (everyone is alert).

- **Long Halt Posture:** Each person takes off their backpack and gets into the prone position in the best covered & concealed position near them, placing their backpack frame down beside them on their support (non-firing hand) side, with the handle facing toward them. This position allows some better rest and protection, while still retaining the ability to move out quickly if needed. In the long halt, it's acceptable to drop to 50% of the people on watch, and 50% fully resting or eating. The backpack could also be used as a weapon support.

Generally, for any stop of less than 15 minutes, you would use the short halt posture. Any longer stops use the long halt posture.

SLLS

Another security tool we have is called the "SLLS". This is a pause of 5-10 minutes to look, listen, and smell for any signs of any human presence (Stop/Look/Listen/Smell). It is done in the short halt posture.

The tendency is to make this too short. Take the time and spend 5-10 actual minutes doing it. What if you stopped for an SLLS at the same time the opposition did? If you got up after only 2 minutes, they know where you are, and you don't know where they are. Invest the time, it could very well save your life.

You can apply this in an urban setting too, and even for individual movement, such as when trying to get home when an event happens. Spending the time becomes even more important when moving alone.

Good times to stop for an SLLS are before and after crossing danger areas, before occupying an overnight stop, right after exiting or just before entering your own perimeter, and generally about once every hour spent moving to rest and refresh, while ensuring your security.

File Formation

The most basic formation is the file formation. Some people call this a "Ranger File" because it sounds cool, but it's really just moving in a single file line. The affiliation with the Rangers comes from the Standing Orders of Rogers' Rangers during the French & Indian War (1759):

When we're on the march, we march single file, far enough apart so one shot can't go through two men.

Major Robert Rogers, 1759

Essentially, the entire group is formed up in a single file line. Each member should be 5-10 meters apart (15-33 feet), for proper dispersion. Being this far apart is quieter and keeps people from getting hit in the face from branches swinging back after the person in front of you moves. It also keeps people focused on paying attention, because they aren't whispering with the next person, and if they aren't paying attention, they might miss a turn. And, as Major Rogers said, one shot can't go through two people.

The person in front, the point person, should be the best person at moving quietly. They are also responsible for navigation in smaller teams.

The rear person is responsible for rear security, but they don't do this by walking backwards. The best way is to adopt a short halt posture briefly, watching behind the formation, then moving. Another way would be to have the two rear people share the responsibility, with one kneeling and watching while the other moves, and then switching.

Everyone else secures to the sides or "flanks". When halting, your team should have a planned procedure, like every other person beginning at the front looking the opposite way.

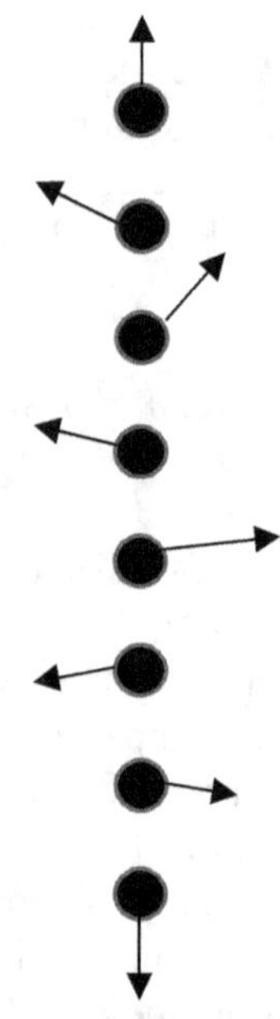

File Formation with Security Sectors

Whenever you halt in the file formation, each person takes 2-3 steps in the direction of their sector before taking a knee behind cover. This will give you an aisle down the center where people can move and still be inside the formation.

Column Formation

The column formation is just 2 files, side by side. Earlier, when we talked about urban team movement, we discussed having half the team on each side of the road; that's the column formation.

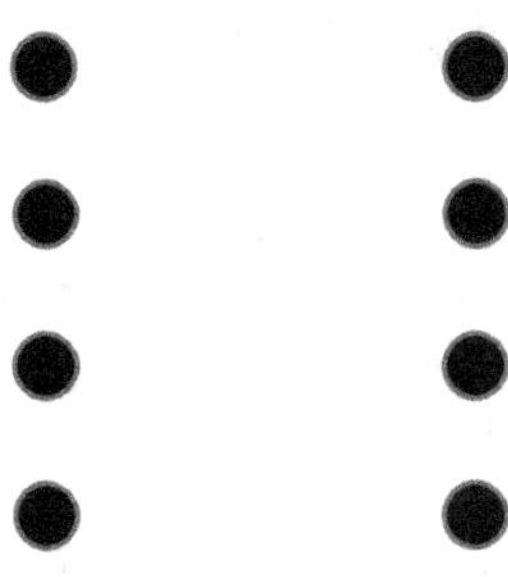

Column Formation

The sectors of observation are the point people focus forward, the rear guards focus behind (this formation lends itself to the bounding pattern we talked about), and the people on the two flanks, watch the flanks on their side. The only exception to this is in urban environment, when the flank security teams will be watching across the street, in upper-level windows, above the other team.

The column formation provides better all-around security than the file but represents a bigger target. It may also make more noise and leave more of a trail.

Line Formation

The last formation for our purposes in this volume is the line formation. This is nothing more than spreading out in a line abreast. It provides great security to the front, but almost none to the flanks or rear.

It would be used if in contact with an opposing force or when preparing to cross a danger area, like a road or trail, to watch the danger area before moving. It's also the basic formation for ambushes, which we will cover in the Scouting & Patrolling volume.

The people on the ends need to watch the flanks, and one person should be designated to turn around and watch the rear.

Line Formation

Team Movement Techniques

There are three basic overall team movement techniques. Your larger group should be broken into at least two units, whether they are fire teams or buddy pairs. These techniques are how these units move in relation to each other.

- Traveling: The teams move together as one unit. It's the least secure but fastest technique.

- Traveling Overwatch: The teams move together but keep a distance of 30-50 meters between them. They move closer together in thick cover and farther apart in open areas.

This ensures that if either team is engaged, the other team is free to maneuver to assist them, and the whole team isn't ambushed at once.

- Bounding Overwatch: This is the most secure method, but it's slow and tiring. One team takes a hardened security position behind cover while the other team moves. The moving team then takes a secured position while the other team moves. You can either have the teams stop abreast of each other (successive bounds) or have them leapfrog, switching which team is in the lead (alternating bounds). This technique is only used when the risk of hostile contact is high.

<u>Recap</u>

Team movement is a complex and detailed skill. Not enough teams spend any time training on it or the reasoning behind it. Proper team movement can help increase your security and survivability, so invest the time in learning how to do it properly.

There are many more advanced formations, and I'm sure the veterans out there will talk about a myriad of others, but these 3 are the foundation for movement. The others are all formations for specific combat patrolling tasks or missions.

Remember the philosophy…first we secure ourselves and our families in a secure and well-defended location. That's the basis for the first two volumes of Tactical Wisdom. Once that's done, we can consider fighting the roving bands of motorcycle gangs like Mad Max or resisting the communist invasion like Red Dawn or even resisting a completely hypothetical tyrannical government.

We have no business learning about ambushes and raids until we know how to move and secure our own base of operations.

<u>Training Standard</u>

- Define a "Buddy Pair".

- Demonstrate the Short Halt Posture.

- Demonstrate the Long Halt Posture.

- Explain what security/observation sectors are.

- Explain the SLLS acronym and when it should be performed.

- Demonstrate the File Formation.

- Demonstrate the Column Formation.

- Demonstrate the Line Formation.

- Explain the three team movement techniques.

Tactical Wisdom

Fieldcraft

Chapter 15

Fieldcraft Tips

The way of fools seems right to them,
but the wise listen to advice.

Proverbs 12:15

We all think we're clever. We think our way is the best, or that we've come up with the greatest idea. It's in our nature to innovate.

Wouldn't it be better instead, as the Ultimate Tactical Handbook advises above, to accept advice hard-won over hundreds of years of Western military experience? Shouldn't we listen to the people who've "been there and done that"?

What I've compiled in this chapter are best practices mainly from the USMC School of Infantry West (because Hollywood Marines are WAY smarter than the Swamp Marines at SOI East) and the Australian Special Air Service Lead Scout program, with some gems from the original fieldcraft experts, Rogers Rangers from the French & Indian War.

These lists aren't all-inclusive, just some of the better suggestions to improve your overall fieldcraft. More will be included in later volumes that apply to specific types of operations.

Australian SAS Lead Scout Tips

- Don't signpost – all trash is either buried or carried out.

- Move with stealth & never at a speed that makes noise.

- Never push on when you are so tired that you can't concentrate, or your alertness is slipping.

- Never look at the ground when moving forward.

- Go around thick brush rather than through; your pack will make noise.

- Never let your weapon be more than an arm's length away.

- Wear your belt kit at all times and have it within arm's reach when sleeping.

- Always use listening halts (SLLS).

- When stopping for a meal halt, leave one person 100 meters back, and then check 100 meters on all sides. It does you no good to sit down to lunch right next to another armed party doing the same thing.

- Put up shelters at last light and be fully ready to move by first light.

- When camping, try to select a site where a surprise night attack would be impossible.

- Don't use trails and try not to leave tracks.

Standing Orders, Rogers' Rangers, 1759

- Have your musket clean as a whistle, hatchet scoured, 60 rounds powder & ball, and be ready to march at a minute's warning (Modern Translation: Keep you weapons clean, a full ammo load, and your gear packed).

- When you're on the march, act the way you would if you were sneaking up on a deer.

- Don't ever take a chance you don't have to.

- When we're on the march we march single file, far enough apart so one shot can't go through two men. (File formation)

- If we strike swamps, or soft ground, we spread out abreast, so it's hard to track us. (Line formation)

- When we march, we keep moving until dark.

- When we camp, half the party stays awake, the other half sleeps.

- Don't ever march home the same way – take a different route so you won't be ambushed.

- Every night, you'll be told where to meet if surrounded by a larger force.

- Don't sit down to eat without posting sentries.

- Don't sleep beyond dawn. Dawn's when the French & Indians attack.

- Don't cross a river by a regular ford.

- Don't stand up when the enemy's coming against you. Kneel down, lie down, hide behind a tree.

There are many more, but these are the most relevant tips, adapted from the Standing Orders of Major Robert Rogers in 1759.

School of Infantry West, USMC

- Every person has a knife and a wristwatch.

- Everyone's gear stays packed at all times.

- Be able to find you gear in the dark, silently and without lights.

- When ending a halt, personnel get up one at a time, rather than all at once.

- Tape everything that makes noise with black or camouflage tape.

- Gear is worn tight to reduce noise.

- When it is very cold outside, keep your compass in an inside pocket to keep the liquid from thickening.

- Buy a supply of burlap and cut it into strips of varying length & width for using as camouflage.

- Camouflage optics and weapons with burlap and rubber bands.

- A small section of camouflage netting can camouflage your ruck/backpack.

- Use small bungee cords to camouflage your belt kit.

- Wet down the dirt in front of your individual position to reduce dust kicked up when firing.

- A mylar blanket camouflaged in your overhead cover can defeat thermal optics.

- When camouflaging a vehicle, cover reflective surfaces like windows with something non-reflective.

- Always keep canteens and water bottles completely full or completely empty to reduce noise.

- In cold weather, store them upside down to prevent the opening from freezing due to exposure.

- Roll up and secure all straps on your ruck/backpack. Use tape or elastic.

- Pack your ruck the same way every time, so that you can always find your gear.

- If your ruck has outer "sustainment pouches": one is used for food and mess gear, the other for rifle cleaning gear & hygiene gear (including wet wipes.

- Inside the ruck, store everything in "kits", like waterproof or Ziploc bags. Have a hygiene kit, a sock kit, an underwear kit.

- Shaving is done in the evening to allow protective oils on your face to replenish overnight.

- Urine can emit a strong odor, so make a small hole, then cover the hole after use.

- Never sleep in wet gear.

- If the enemy is known to be close, wear boots while sleeping. If not, place them next to you, but cover them to prevent animals and insects from entering.

- All gear is packed away before sleeping each night.

- Don't wear hoods or cover ears with hats when listening.

- Metal on metal sounds are inherently man made.

- Smoking ruins your sense of smell and can be detected from a very long way off. At night it can be seen as well.

Training Standard

- Be able to recite at least 5 Fieldcraft Tips and put them into practice.

Tactical Wisdom

Fieldcraft

Warrior Study: David

Once again, these both first appeared as blog posts at tactical-wisdom.com, where I discuss preparedness issues from the perspective of the Ultimate Tactical Handbook.

They are presented here to give classic examples of the tactics in this book, their link to the Ultimate Tactical Handbook, and finally to show that they are just as valid today.

Tactics - David in the Desert of Ziph

Modern tactics are really nothing more than the same tactics used for thousands of years, just re-written to sound more high-tech. It was once said that it was the longbow, and not the infantryman that became obsolete, and the horse, not the cavalryman. That is very true.

However, the same combat engineer and security skills that Nehemiah used in Jerusalem are still in use today, as are the same recon skills and tactics that David used in the Desert of Ziph, thousands of years ago.

In 1 Samuel 26, a great adventure story plays out that proves that the Bible is still the Ultimate Tactical Handbook. Let me set the stage.

King Saul knew that David was going to replace him some day, so
he decided to kill David. David had already survived a few
assassination attempts. David and his small band of warriors were
hiding out in the wilderness of the Desert of Ziph.

King Saul brought 3,000 troops and because the force was so large,
they had to camp right beside the road…. You can't hide 3,000
men without making a trail. These two pieces are the first tactical
lessons in this story.

- Don't bring a massive force to search for a small force, it's
  very easy to track, and hard to hide.

- Don't set up or halt in an obvious danger zone, where you
  can be found or observed easily.

When David heard that Saul was near, he immediately sent out
scouts, who fixed the location of Saul's forces and reported back to
David. Two more quick tactical points that are equally valid today:

- Have an intelligence network up and running, so that you
  hear about things happening. Because David had a
  network, his team immediately knew when a threat was
  near.

- Confirm all reports by getting your own people to
  physically observe what's been reported. David could
  have launched an attack as soon as he heard, but what if
  Saul wasn't really there? David would have exposed his
  meager force.

Once David's scouts reported back to the main body where the
enemy was, David immediately went to take a look himself and

finalize a plan. Today, we give that the fancy name of "Leader's Reconnaissance", but despite the modern name, it's the same thing David did.

- Conduct a Leader's Recon to finalize your plans. David took one other man with him, for security, you should too.

- When leaving on a Leader's Recon, issue a "GOTWA" plan.

    o Going: Where you are going

    o Others: Who is going with you

    o Time: Time of your return

    o What: What to do if you don't return

    o Actions: What to do if you are attacked or the main body is attacked during the recon.

Now, David and his partner were able to sneak into the enemy camp undetected because the King's forces were confident that no one would attack a force of 3,000.

- ALWAYS post security and have a security and sleep plan for your entire team.

David found where the King was sleeping, and the King's spear and water jug were sitting near his head. Rather than killing the King, which would have meant a victory, for about 2 seconds until the other 3,000 men woke up and killed David, David disarmed the King and took his water jug.

- Fighting is not always the best option.

- Sometimes, removing resources from an enemy force can force it to retire or lose (The Crusader "Army of God" lost the Battle of Hattin in 1187 because of a lack of water).

David and his escort then withdrew but continued in a direction AWAY from their own forces and secured themselves a position on a hill overlooking the enemy camp.

- Use deception by traveling in an unexpected direction or by leading pursuers away from your true positions.

- Always secure high ground and commanding terrain (There was a river as an obstacle).

- Use the Acronym KOCOA to pick out the best position:

  - Key Terrain

  - Observation & Fields of Fire

  - Cover & Concealment

  - Obstacles

  - Avenues of approach

The next morning, David contacted the enemy force and let them know that he had penetrated their camp and could have killed their King in his sleep but chose not to. The King was shaken by this and saw it as a sign. The King immediately vowed to stop pursuing

David. While we know that outcome isn't certain in today's world, it does give us a couple of tactical points.

- Sometimes, simply making it known that you COULD have acted, but instead showed FORBEARANCE accomplishes far more than fighting.

- In preparedness, not every fight is a fight we SHOULD make. In fact, we should avoid it as much as possible.

Now, that's a fun analysis that illustrated some very basic tactical principles, but how does that apply to preparedness?

Most people who are into preparedness want to immediately talk about all the guns they have and all the tactical training they do, but that misses the entire point of preparedness.

The point of preparedness is to SURVIVE. Sure, being able to fend off an attack is a good skill to have, but it's not always the best option.

You aren't going to be light infantry out in the outback with Mad Max, righting the wrongs of society.

This story illustrates that by applying proper tactics, and accomplishing your goals WITHOUT fighting, you'll be a lot better off in the long run. Sure, David could have been all secret-squirrel ninja and killed the King, but how would he have gotten out of the camp, and then away from the pursuit that was sure to follow? His 600 men would not have fared well against 3,000.

By not fighting, he solved the problem on a far more permanent basis. Let that be the one tactical truth you take away from here.

He was not showing weakness; remember that at this point, David was already known as a great Warrior. He showed STRENGTH by choosing not to destroy the King.

There is a great lesson in that.

The other lesson I hope people take away from this analysis of David's tactics in the Desert of Ziph is that your training shouldn't always involve punching holes in paper. The ability to conduct Scouting & Patrolling, operate a Listening/Observation Post, and how to gather intelligence are all skills that anyone into preparedness should master, even more than shooting.

Tactical History – The Sack of Ziklag

This is an epic battle story and a classic study of tactics that directly applies to us as people interested in preparedness. It highlights some pieces of Tactical Wisdom that are vital to our plans for a WROL situation and happens to be a pretty cool story.

If anyone wants to follow along, the full tale can be found in 1 Samuel 27-30.

For a little historical context, before he became King of Israel, David was much like us. He joined his Nation's army and fought for them, killing one of its greatest enemies. But much like the purge we are seeing in our military and the targeting of our veteran's, as soon as the war was over, the King turned on David, labeled him an extremist and hunted him down.

In fact, drawing yet another parallel to today, the King invited him into the palace, then tried to kill him, and sent agents to raid his house, but he escaped out a window.

David was then branded as a rebel, a resistance fighter. He eventually formed his own militia, and they spent their days avoiding the government agents, while still protecting their country. Does that sound familiar?

Today's story begins when David has founded a private military company with his 600 men. They are called "mercenaries" in 1 Samuel 27, but their job was securing the borders for the Philistine King. King Achish named David his "bodyguard for life" and set him up with a base in the village of Ziklag.

King Achish decides to go to war against Israel, and David accompanies him. Here, we see some parallels to today that we must face. David does NOT want to fight against his own country, but he feels he needs to be near the fighting to try and slow down the decline. David loved his Nation, but the leader had turned from the path of the country and was imposing his own will on the people, rather than following tradition. Does that sound familiar?

At this point, David knew that the leadership had to go, but he didn't want to destroy the Nation. Here are the truths we know and need to consider:

- It's possible to love your Nation but know that the leadership is leading it to destruction.

- When that happens, you must consider what is worse.... the short-term pain of action, or the long-term consequence of doing nothing.

- Readiness is key - David kept his 600 men ready by training and engaging in operations that didn't directly oppose his nation but kept his Warriors on the edge they needed.

- Avoiding conflict can help, but it won't solve it - David and his force spent 3-4 years before these events evading and avoiding contact with government forces. Nothing improved.

Back to the tale at hand...

As the Philistine (Palestinian) forces began to invade Israel (a lot of that going on even today), they brought their entire army out, leaving no one behind. The other generals were freaked out by an Israelite private military company in their midst, and they were so worried that they demanded the King send David home.

So, the King went to David and said "Listen, I know you've served me well, fighting a counter-insurgency on my borders, but I can't have a radical like you around." And he sent David home. David and his Warriors were livid. They had fought in two different wars successfully, and were now being branded as extremists, and a security risk. They turned around and headed home.

Lessons here:

- Alienating trained and effective warriors who have served you well is DANGEROUS.

- If David and his men weren't radicalized yet, their treatment by the new government certainly did radicalize them. (Hmm....)

As the men neared their compound in Ziklag, they found it burning. Everything they had left behind was stolen, including their wives and children. A few more towns nearby had also been sacked and they received information that it was the people they had been fighting before. David and his men took off in pursuit. Of course, David first asked God for guidance, and God told him to go, essentially saying "What are you waiting for?"

- Leaving your rear area unguarded and your base of operations undefended will lead to disaster EVERY SINGLE TIME.

- The way of life at the time is how we envision WROL life to be. Our base of operations will be where our food is produced, our livestock will be, and where are our families will be. There will be bands of bandits about. It must be guarded by an effective force at all times.

David and his men gave pursuit, but carrying their supplies was wearing them out and slowing them down. David detailed 200 of his men to stay with the slower-moving supply trains, while the other 400 rushed on ahead.

Soon, they found a straggler from the enemy force wandering in the desert. They fed him and asked for information. It turned out that he was a slave who had escaped. In exchange for protection and food, the slave led them to the enemy camp.

David and his men assaulted the camp and after a 2-day battle, they had destroyed most of the enemy force, and the rest was fleeing headlong back to Egypt. They had rescued all their family members, and gained not only their own property back, but the raiding force's extra supplies and plunder from other towns.

On the way back, they met up with the logistical tail, and David's 400 didn't want to share to any of the plunder or extra supplies with the 200 that guarded the supply trains. David pointed out that the entire chain of events was a lesson. That lesson was that guarding your supply chain was every bit as vital as winning the battle against the enemy and he ordered that the security troops be given a full share.

Lessons in the end:

- You cannot succeed without securing your logistics.

- Supplies need to be guarded by a substantial force.

- Security is the most important task.

- Never leave your base (and food and families) undefended by an effective force.

- Attempt to gather intelligence from everyone you meet (the wandering slave).

The most important lesson here is that Warriors who love their Nation and fought for it should never be neglected or treated as extremists. They can love their Nation and hate its leadership. Alienating them never leads to a good place.

The other lesson is that we need to focus on securing our families and supplies first, then worry about other objectives, which is a concept I mention in both Tactical Wisdom books.

www.ingramcontent.com/pod-product-compliance
Lightning Source LLC
Chambersburg PA
CBHW061343250726

48657CB00004B/1308